# OREGON
## A STATE THAT **STANDS OUT**

*For more information on this book scan this QR Code*

Copyright © 2016 by Michael McCloskey
Cover and interior design by Emily Coats

Publisher's Cataloging-in-Publication data

    McCloskey, J. Michael (John Michael), t- author.
      Oregon : a state that stands out / by Michael McCloskey.
      pages cm
      Includes bibliographical references.
      LCCN 2016900749
      ISBN 978-1-62901-338-1(pbk.)
      ISBN 978-1-62901-339-8 (Kindle ebk)

    1. Oregon--History.    I. Title.

F876.M383 2016        979.5
                        QBI16-600053

All rights reserved. Except where explicitly stated, no part of this book may be reproduced or transmitted in any form or by any means whatsoever, including photocopying, recording or by any information storage and retrieval system, without written permission from the publisher and/or author.

Publisher: Inkwater Press

Paperback
ISBN-13 978-1-62901-338-1 | ISBN-10 1-62901-338-2

Kindle
ISBN-13 978-1-62901-339-8 | ISBN-10 1-62901-339-0

1    3    5    7    9    10    8    6    4    2

# OREGON
## A STATE THAT **STANDS OUT**

Michael McCloskey

PORTLAND•OREGON
INKWATERPRESS.COM

# CONTENTS

ACNOWLEDGEMENTS . . . . . . . . . . . . . . . . . . . . . . . . 1
INTRODUCTION. . . . . . . . . . . . . . . . . . . . . . . . . . . . . 3

**CHAPTER 1**  NOTABLE HISTORIC POINTS. . . . . . . . . . . . . 6
   The Oregon Trail and Exploration of Oregon . . . . . . . . . . . . . . . . 6
   Settlement of Oregon. . . . . . . . . . . . . . . . . . . . . . . . . . . . . . . . . . . 9
   Various Firsts in the Oregon Country. . . . . . . . . . . . . . . . . . . . . 11
   Early Shipbuilding in Oregon . . . . . . . . . . . . . . . . . . . . . . . . . . . 12

**CHAPTER 2**  DEVELOPMENT FIRSTS . . . . . . . . . . . . . . . . .13

**CHAPTER 3**  RECORD-SETTING FEATURES . . . . . . . . . . .18

**CHAPTER 4**  THINGS THAT GIVE
OREGON CHARACTER . . . . . . . . . . . . . . . . . . . . . . . . . . . . . . . .29
   Odds and Ends . . . . . . . . . . . . . . . . . . . . . . . . . . . . . . . . . . . . . . 35

**CHAPTER 5**  GOVERNANCE . . . . . . . . . . . . . . . . . . . . . . . .48
   Leader in Reforms of the Progressive Era . . . . . . . . . . . . . . . . . . 48
   Leadership in Later Reforms (post-Progressive Era) . . . . . . . . . . 51
   Other Information about Governance . . . . . . . . . . . . . . . . . . . . 53

**CHAPTER 6** GEOGRAPHIC FEATURES . . . . . . . . . . . . . . . . . 55
   Water . . . . . . . . . . . . . . . . . . . . . . . . . . . . . . . . . . . . . . . . . . . . . . . . . 55
   Volcanic Activity . . . . . . . . . . . . . . . . . . . . . . . . . . . . . . . . . . . . . . . 56
   Other Geologic Forces / Miscellany . . . . . . . . . . . . . . . . . . . . . . . . 57
   Coastline . . . . . . . . . . . . . . . . . . . . . . . . . . . . . . . . . . . . . . . . . . . . . . 58
   Biology . . . . . . . . . . . . . . . . . . . . . . . . . . . . . . . . . . . . . . . . . . . . . . . 59
   Celebrated Gardens . . . . . . . . . . . . . . . . . . . . . . . . . . . . . . . . . . . . . 64

**CHAPTER 7** ENVIRONMENTAL CONVERSATION . . . . . . . . 67
   Environment . . . . . . . . . . . . . . . . . . . . . . . . . . . . . . . . . . . . . . . . . . 67
   Conservation . . . . . . . . . . . . . . . . . . . . . . . . . . . . . . . . . . . . . . . . . . 70

**CHAPTER 8** NATURAL RESOURCES AND AGRICULTURE . . . . 73
   Forest Products . . . . . . . . . . . . . . . . . . . . . . . . . . . . . . . . . . . . . . . . 73
   Farms and Fisheries . . . . . . . . . . . . . . . . . . . . . . . . . . . . . . . . . . . . 74
   Wines, Olive Oil, and Cheeses . . . . . . . . . . . . . . . . . . . . . . . . . . . . 75
   Specialty Crops . . . . . . . . . . . . . . . . . . . . . . . . . . . . . . . . . . . . . . . . 76
   Nurseries and Flowers . . . . . . . . . . . . . . . . . . . . . . . . . . . . . . . . . . 78

**CHAPTER 9** SOCIAL MATTERS . . . . . . . . . . . . . . . . . . . . . . . 80
   Health . . . . . . . . . . . . . . . . . . . . . . . . . . . . . . . . . . . . . . . . . . . . . . . 80
   Education . . . . . . . . . . . . . . . . . . . . . . . . . . . . . . . . . . . . . . . . . . . . 82
   Religion . . . . . . . . . . . . . . . . . . . . . . . . . . . . . . . . . . . . . . . . . . . . . . 83
   Charity . . . . . . . . . . . . . . . . . . . . . . . . . . . . . . . . . . . . . . . . . . . . . . . 84
   Crime and Incarceration . . . . . . . . . . . . . . . . . . . . . . . . . . . . . . . . 85

**CHAPTER 10** OREGON'S ROLE IN WARS . . . . . . . . . . . . . . . 86
   Civil War . . . . . . . . . . . . . . . . . . . . . . . . . . . . . . . . . . . . . . . . . . . . . 86
   Spanish-American War . . . . . . . . . . . . . . . . . . . . . . . . . . . . . . . . . . 87
   World War I . . . . . . . . . . . . . . . . . . . . . . . . . . . . . . . . . . . . . . . . . . 87
   Inter-War Period . . . . . . . . . . . . . . . . . . . . . . . . . . . . . . . . . . . . . . . 87
   World War II . . . . . . . . . . . . . . . . . . . . . . . . . . . . . . . . . . . . . . . . . . 88

**CHAPTER 11**  HISTORIC PRESERVATION . . . . . . . . . . . . . .91
    Hotels . . . . . . . . . . . . . . . . . . . . . . . . . . . . . . . . . . . . . . . 91
    Failures . . . . . . . . . . . . . . . . . . . . . . . . . . . . . . . . . . . . . . 92
    Historic Movie Theaters. . . . . . . . . . . . . . . . . . . . . . . . . . 93
    Other Commercial Buildings. . . . . . . . . . . . . . . . . . . . . . . 95
    Civic Buildings . . . . . . . . . . . . . . . . . . . . . . . . . . . . . . . . 96
    Other Buildings. . . . . . . . . . . . . . . . . . . . . . . . . . . . . . . . 99
    Elsewhere in the State . . . . . . . . . . . . . . . . . . . . . . . . . . 100

**CHAPTER 12**  SAFE DRIVING AND CAR DATA . . . . . . . . 107

**CHAPTER 13**  BUSINESS AND THE ECONOMY . . . . . . . . 109
    A Place to Do Business . . . . . . . . . . . . . . . . . . . . . . . . . 109
    Worker Well-Being . . . . . . . . . . . . . . . . . . . . . . . . . . . . 111
    Business History . . . . . . . . . . . . . . . . . . . . . . . . . . . . . . 112
    Largest or Best of Its Kind . . . . . . . . . . . . . . . . . . . . . . . 115
    Well-Known Businesses . . . . . . . . . . . . . . . . . . . . . . . . 118
    Firms Supporting Aviation. . . . . . . . . . . . . . . . . . . . . . . 121
    Unique Products . . . . . . . . . . . . . . . . . . . . . . . . . . . . . 126
    Attracting Attention. . . . . . . . . . . . . . . . . . . . . . . . . . . 127
    **High-Tech Industries** (including the "Silicon Forest" and Intel) . . . . . . 128
    The Rest of Silicon Forest. . . . . . . . . . . . . . . . . . . . . . . . 131
    Other High-Tech Industries. . . . . . . . . . . . . . . . . . . . . . 132
    Environmental Industries. . . . . . . . . . . . . . . . . . . . . . . . 135

**CHAPTER 14**  ARTS, CULTURE,
AND ENTERTAINMENT . . . . . . . . . . . . . . . . . . . . . . . . . 138
    Arts and Culture . . . . . . . . . . . . . . . . . . . . . . . . . . . . . 138
    Popular Entertainment. . . . . . . . . . . . . . . . . . . . . . . . . 142
    Food and Drink. . . . . . . . . . . . . . . . . . . . . . . . . . . . . . 144
    Miscellaneous . . . . . . . . . . . . . . . . . . . . . . . . . . . . . . . 145

Well-Known People Who Have Lived in Oregon . . . . . . . . . . . . . . . . . . 149
Films, Television Programs, and Novels Set in Oregon . . . . . . . . . . . . . 151
Songs Featuring Oregon. . . . . . . . . . . . . . . . . . . . . . . . . . . . . . . . . . . 152

**CHAPTER 15** UNIVERSITIES IN OREGON: STANDING AND ACCOMPLISHMENTS . . . . . . . . . . . . . . . . . . . . . . . . . . . . . . . . . . . . . . . 154
Oregon Health & Science University (OHSU). . . . . . . . . . . . . . . . . . . 154
Oregon State University (OSU) . . . . . . . . . . . . . . . . . . . . . . . . . . . . . 154
University of Oregon (U of O). . . . . . . . . . . . . . . . . . . . . . . . . . . . . . 155
Reed College (Portland). . . . . . . . . . . . . . . . . . . . . . . . . . . . . . . . . . 156
Portland State University (PSU) . . . . . . . . . . . . . . . . . . . . . . . . . . . . 157
Oregon Institute of Technology (Wilsonville). . . . . . . . . . . . . . . . . . . 157
Lewis & Clark College. . . . . . . . . . . . . . . . . . . . . . . . . . . . . . . . . . . 157
University of Portland . . . . . . . . . . . . . . . . . . . . . . . . . . . . . . . . . . . 158
Willamette University (Salem) . . . . . . . . . . . . . . . . . . . . . . . . . . . . . 158
Pacific University (Forest Grove) . . . . . . . . . . . . . . . . . . . . . . . . . . . 158
Linfield College (McMinnville) . . . . . . . . . . . . . . . . . . . . . . . . . . . . 158
George Fox University (Newberg) . . . . . . . . . . . . . . . . . . . . . . . . . . 158

**CHAPTER 16** ACHIEVEMENT IN SPORTS . . . . . . . . . . . . . . 159
Football. . . . . . . . . . . . . . . . . . . . . . . . . . . . . . . . . . . . . . . . . . . . . . 159
Baseball . . . . . . . . . . . . . . . . . . . . . . . . . . . . . . . . . . . . . . . . . . . . . 161
Basketball . . . . . . . . . . . . . . . . . . . . . . . . . . . . . . . . . . . . . . . . . . . . 162
Track and Field . . . . . . . . . . . . . . . . . . . . . . . . . . . . . . . . . . . . . . . . 163
Miscellaneous . . . . . . . . . . . . . . . . . . . . . . . . . . . . . . . . . . . . . . . . . 165
Golf. . . . . . . . . . . . . . . . . . . . . . . . . . . . . . . . . . . . . . . . . . . . . . . . . 165
Hockey . . . . . . . . . . . . . . . . . . . . . . . . . . . . . . . . . . . . . . . . . . . . . . 166
Rodeo Riding . . . . . . . . . . . . . . . . . . . . . . . . . . . . . . . . . . . . . . . . . 166
Soccer . . . . . . . . . . . . . . . . . . . . . . . . . . . . . . . . . . . . . . . . . . . . . . 167
Swimming. . . . . . . . . . . . . . . . . . . . . . . . . . . . . . . . . . . . . . . . . . . . 167

    Surfing. . . . . . . . . . . . . . . . . . . . . . . . . . . . . . . . . . . . . . . . . . 168
    Tennis . . . . . . . . . . . . . . . . . . . . . . . . . . . . . . . . . . . . . . . . . . . 168
    Skiing, Snowboarding, and Sled Racing . . . . . . . . . . . . . . . . . . . 169
    Mountain and Rock Climbing . . . . . . . . . . . . . . . . . . . . . . . . . . . 170
    Windsurfing and Hang Gliding . . . . . . . . . . . . . . . . . . . . . . . . . . 170
    Angling . . . . . . . . . . . . . . . . . . . . . . . . . . . . . . . . . . . . . . . . . . 171
    Distinctive Fishing Boats Developed in Oregon: . . . . . . . . . . . . . . 171
CONCLUSIONS . . . . . . . . . . . . . . . . . . . . . . . . . . . . . . . . . 173
SOURCES . . . . . . . . . . . . . . . . . . . . . . . . . . . . . . . . . . . . . 175
INDEX. . . . . . . . . . . . . . . . . . . . . . . . . . . . . . . . . . . . . . . 177

# ACNOWLEDGEMENTS

A number of people have helped me shape this book. I developed the approach in conversations with Elaine Friedman and Sue and Mike Malter. I am grateful to them for the time they time spent in helping me move the ideas along.

Others were kind enough to read drafts and offer me helpful feedback. These included Sidney Herbert, Laura King, Chris Williams, Jennifer Harrington, and my brother and my niece: David and Amanda McCloskey.

Once again, Jim McMullen was very helpful in taking expert photographs, as well as acquiring others from various sources. And Chris Williams helped me with computer operations.

Many thanks to all of these people. I hope they like the final result.

And my special thanks go to those who have offered helpful endorsements.

Michael McCloskey

**NOTE TO THE READER:** in this text, notable items that explain why Oregon stands out are marked in **bold**.

# INTRODUCTION

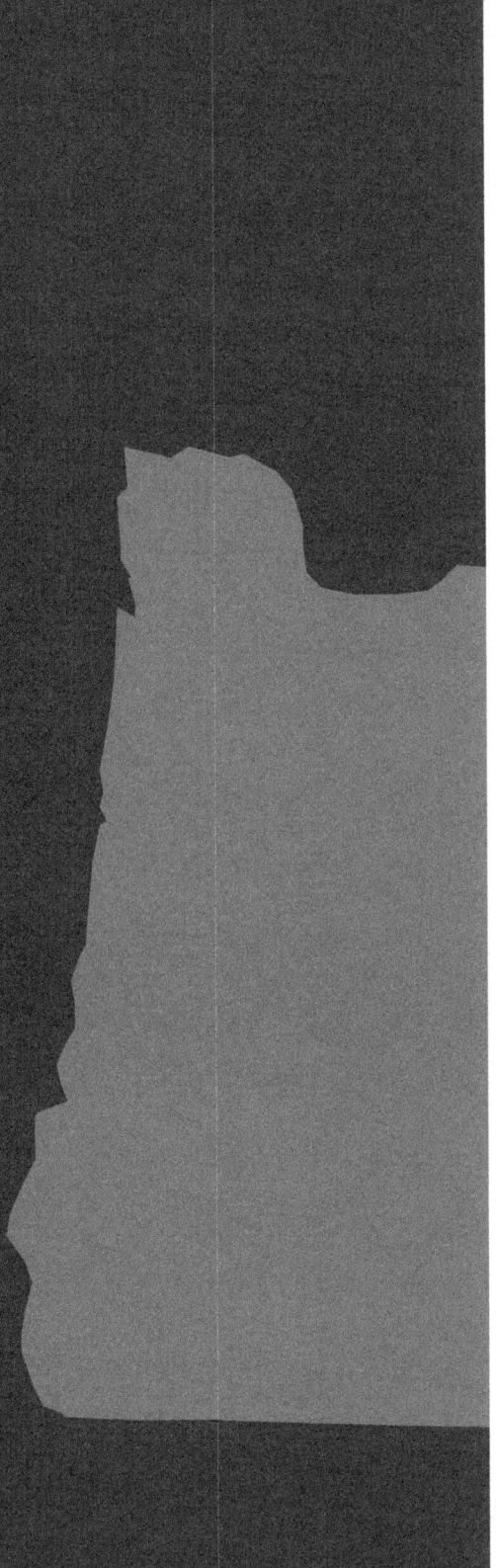

Some states stand out because they are large—some because they are populous. Some are memorable because historically important things have happened there.

But some are distinguished by what is there, by what is being done in them, or by the quality of life there. Oregon is such a state. It stands out because of what it is.

Moreover, Oregon stands out because it has character—interesting things have happened here. Things in the West often began here.

This book features many points of this kind about Oregon, grouped together by categories. These are the kind of things that cause Oregon to stand out when viewed nationally (rather than just being Oregon's best).

To be more specific, things are listed here for various reasons:

- Oregon was the first in the West to have them;
- Oregon led the nation in getting them;
- they lend character to the state;
- they have been the best in the nation; or
- things produced here have been sold all over the country, or even the world.

This book does not cover undertakings that are merely ordinary. It is highly selective in what it mentions.

The book aims to
- deepen the interest that residents take in their state;
- promote understanding of how impressive the state's record is;
- generate pride in the state, and determination to continue excelling;
- motivate Oregonians to try harder to overcome the shortcomings which remain; and
- demonstrate that a healthy environment can go together with a healthy economy.

A business section is included to help make this last point. This section
- documents the investment that Oregon has made in a modern economy;
- casts light on what a modern economy looks like;
- demonstrates the breadth, variety, and depth of Oregon's involvement in that economy, as well as its staying power; and
- is presented after data on the state's natural endowment and its commitment to high environmental standards, showing that the two now coexist and are compatible.

Sometimes this modern economy is characterized as the "New Economy." In Oregon, it is composed of high technology businesses, aviation, fabrication of specialized metal and composite products, the nursery trade, specialty crops, athletics and athletic products, and elements in health services, education, and the arts and culture.

The New Economy represents a move away from what many have characterized as the "Old Economy": the process of extracting natural resources seen in such industries as logging, ranching, mining, commercial fishing, and traditional farming. In Oregon, this transition has already occurred, although there are remnants of the extractive economy and they continue to cause environmental problems.

When we examine this transition, two other profound perspectives emerge. First, the cumulative record of Oregon's achievements shows that high standards and leadership have emerged again and again. And second, this record is particularly amazing in light of the limited size of Oregon's population. On a per capita basis, Oregon often compares well (on matters of food and culture, for instance) with states that are much larger. And it has often led the way in making improvements in social welfare and environmental policy.

Certainly, not everything that now goes on in the state rises to high levels, and not everything in its past is admirable. But more and more of what goes on here today does stand out, and for the most part the state has overcome the ignoble moments in its past. And in general, it has built upon the admirable things in its past.

In sum, Oregon not only stands out again and again, it must be viewed as a place of distinction—in contrast to historian Gordon Dodd's conclusion, forty years ago, that too often "Oregon…[has been] satisfied with the competent, not the distinguished." That no longer seems to be true. That is worth celebrating!

# CHAPTER I

# NOTABLE HISTORIC POINTS

## THE OREGON TRAIL AND EXPLORATION OF OREGON

The quest to come to Oregon in the 1840s was called "Oregon Fever." The migration of Euro-Americans along the Oregon Trail, in the twenty years between 1840-1860, is recognized as one of the largest voluntary migrations in the history of the world.[1] Over this time, over 300,000 people trekked westward along portions of this trail to various western states. Some ten percent perished in the process (mainly from accidents and disease). It is estimated that 53,000 then found their way to Oregon.

Of the various trails to the West Coast, the route to Oregon was the longest—2000 miles.

Settlement of Oregon was preceded by three centuries of exploration by other nations. The Spanish were the first to show interest, looking closely at our coastline as its mariners passed by. But notwithstanding the fact that Spanish names stud the Oregon coastline, the Spanish flag never flew here.

Coastal sightings of Oregon by European explorers began in 1543, with Juan Rodriguez Cabrillo and Bartolome Ferrelo. And then in 1603 Cape Sebastian was seen by Sebastian Vizciano. For a few centuries after 1565, Spanish galleons coming from the Philippines rode the Japanese current east across the north Pacific to pass by the Oregon coast on their way to Mexico. Some visited (some involuntarily), and relics and shipwrecks remain (e.g., the *San Francis Xavier*, which wrecked in 1707 at Nehalem spit).

In 1774, Juan Perez Hernandez discovered Yaquina Head. In 1775, Bruno de Heceta found the mouth of the Columbia River (on his way back to his southerly base). Heceta Head is named after him.

Various Spanish names along Oregon's coast stem from these visits: Cape Ferrelo, Cape Blanco,[2] Cape Sebastian, Heceta Head, Cape Falcon, and Yaquina Head.

In 1819, Spain ceded all of its discovery rights in Oregon (i.e., north of what is now the California line).

Notwithstanding a substantial amount of British exploration here and a period of joint control (1818-1846), Great Britain never had undisputed control of Oregon.

That country's claims grew out of a long record of British exploration. It is even possible that Sir Francis Drake observed the Oregon coast in 1579, while circumnavigating the globe. Some also believe he stopped at Nehalem Bay to repair his ship.

British explorer Captain James Cook explored the Oregon coast in 1778 (sighting Cape Arago), and made landfall near Cape Foulweather, which he named. In 1788-9, British captain John Meares also explored the Oregon coast (Cape Meares is named after him). He originally tried to name it Cape Lookout, but that name is now applied to the most prominent cape on the coast, which is ten miles to the south.

In 1792, Captain George Vancouver and Lieutenant William Broughton explored the lower Columbia River, crossing the bar at last. Vancouver concluded this trip by sailing down the coast to turn around south of Cape Blanco. American Captain Robert Gray had also crossed the bar—just days before.

In 1813, the British took over an outpost at Astoria (it had been started two years before by John Jacob Astor's Pacific Fur Company) and named it Fort George. It was then taken over by the Northwest Fur Company. **Astoria was the first permanent English-speaking settlement west of the Rockies.**

[1] The phrase "voluntary migration" excludes refugees from war, persecution, famine, and epidemics.

[2] The spectacular white cliffs around Cape Blanco were noted by a Spanish explorer in 1603.

*Notable Historic Points*

The Hudson Bay Company (HBC), led by Dr. John McLoughlin, dominated trading in the Columbia River territory from 1821-1846. It was based in what is now Vancouver, Washington. The company's operations had a deep impact on what is now the state of Oregon, particularly in the Willamette Valley. Their brigades organized systematic efforts to trap beavers, and explored and mapped much of the region. In 1832, British trappers established Fort Umpqua at Elkton (on the lower Umpqua River); this was the most southerly base of the HBC.

HBC explorer/trapper Peter Skene Ogden passed through the Rogue River valley in the 1820s. HBC's Alexander Roderick McLeod traveled the middle of the Oregon coast in the same period—as did Donald McKenzie, who trapped his way through Lane County.

David Douglas botanized western Oregon in 1826, discovering the Sugar pine species near present-day Roseburg. He sent seeds of what we now know as the Douglas fir to England. Many species common to Oregon are named after him.

After a while, Dr. McLoughlin made his home in Oregon City. At most of their outposts, HBC employees planted gardens, orchards, and raised livestock—thereby testing the agricultural potential of the country (including at Sauvie Island in 1841).

American claims to Oregon were most solidly based on the migration of US settlers that began in the 1830s—though its claims were also based on a credible record of exploration. Captain Robert Gray had visited Tillamook Bay to trade in 1788, and then was **the first explorer to enter the Columbia River**, which he did in 1792. And then there was the expedition of Lewis and Clark; the establishment of Fort Clatsop (1805) and Fort Astoria (1811); the Wilson Price Hunt expedition to Astoria (1811) and the ill-fated ship *Tonquin* (which sank that same year); and finally the visits of Capt. John Biddle (1818). Trappers from the American Fur Company began to enter Deschutes County in 1813. In due course these included Kit Carson and Nathaniel J. Wyeth. Captain B.L.E. Bonneville visited Wallowa County in 1834.

Boosters in places such as Boston began promoting colonization of what was then called "the Oregon country" as early as the 1820s. In 1830, Hall J. Kelley in Boston published a book describing the geography and promise of the region.

By the 1840s, the fur trade had begun to decline. Beaver had been trapped out, and the demand for fur hats declined with changing fashions. Various authors, such as Washington Irving, popularized interest in the Oregon country and the trips of explorers who had been here. People were also reading the works of various naturalists who had visited the region. In 1840, Robert Greenow composed a report for the US State Department, setting forth the case for an American claim on Oregon.

Now the focus shifted to the agricultural potential of specific places in the Oregon country—such as the Willamette Valley, with its moderate climate, which was praised for that reason by Lt. Charles Wilkes during an 1841 expedition. In 1842, John Fremont explored eastern Oregon (among other areas).

## SETTLEMENT OF OREGON

When the settlers first began to arrive in numbers, in most places few natives remained. By 1800, ninety percent of them had died from diseases brought by traders and trappers. In most places, little conflict arose between settlers and the handful of remaining natives.

The largest early agricultural settlements in the Northwest were made in the 1830s at Oregon's French Prairie (the area between Portland and Salem). The first settlers there were retired French-Canadian fur trappers, who married native women and raised families and farmed. Subsequently, American settlers, attracted by the local Methodist mission, came into the area just north of today's Salem.

Catholic clergy came to French Prairie to serve the families of the retired French-Canadian fur trappers. While neither the Catholics nor the Methodists had much success in converting natives, these missionaries did pave the way for more settlers.

*Notable Historic Points*

In 1843, settlers decided by only one vote to try to become part of the United States rather than the British empire, at a conclave at Champoeg on the French Prairie.

The provisional government in Oregon was organized in 1843 at Champoeg—becoming the **first acting public government of Americans in the Oregon country**. Up until then, governmental functions had been handled in Vancouver by the Hudson Bay Company. The northern boundary of the new provisional government of Oregon was the Columbia River.

The provisional government set up a legislature, with a governor (George Abernathy), and adopted laws based on those from the state of Iowa (as a matter of happenstance, someone had a law book from that state). They adopted laws to handle such things as wills and property. They also set bounties, established courts, collected taxes, built roads and bridges, and ran ferries. They used hides, lard, and lumber (among other things) as legal tender—lacking any better option.

They also formed a militia—taking hostile action against some natives, and hanging anyone who challenged the laws of the provisional government. The militia, which was formed in 1843, initially consisted of companies of mounted riflemen, and was directed by a major and three captains. One of these companies, consisting of twenty-five men under the command of Captain T. D. Keysur, was used to put down rebellions of those resisting the new regime.

In 1847, when 14 settlers were killed in the Whitman Massacre, Governor Abernathy sent a company of 45 mounted riflemen, under the command of Captain H.A.G. Lee, to pursue the natives who had attacked. They were known as the "Oregon Rifles." They were successful in what came to be known as the Cayuse War. Later that year, Abernathy appointed an Adjutant General and a colonel to command the provincial government's regiment.

In 1839 a writer in the book *Pacific Republic* forecast that the Oregon territory might be destined to become an independent republic. (In 1860, governor Joseph Lane even tried to lead Oregon out of the union and into something he called "the Pacific Republic of the Western States"—a move favored by southern sympathizers.)

## VARIOUS FIRSTS IN THE OREGON COUNTRY

Since Oregon was the site of the first US settlements on the West Coast, many national "firsts" happened there.

**Oregon City was the first city west of the Missouri River to be incorporated** (a process that occurred in 1844). The city became the seat of the provisional government.

The first taxes to be collected from Americans on the West Coast came from those living in Oregon in 1844 and were paid to the provisional government operating there.

This provisional government was anxious to get US mail service and secure military backing, as well as other services. In 1848 Joe Meek (a retired mountain man/trapper, who became an early tax collector) and friends took a memorial—a petition to the federal government authorized by the provincial government—back to Washington, D.C., asking for these services, as well as explaining the need for revenue laws and a way to deal with land claims. In his exuberant way, Meek introduced himself as "an envoy and minister plenipotentiary from the republic of Oregon." Before long, the US government responded favorably.

The **first territorial government of the United States** on the West Coast was established in Oregon in 1848; Oregon City was its capital. The Oregon Exchange Company minted 6000 "Beaver Coins" (in 5 and 10 dollar denominations) for that territorial government, beginning in 1849.

The government's flag had a yellow beaver in a field of blue on its backside. It was the **only governmental entity to have a flag with different designs on each side**. Oregon did not get around to adopting an official flag until 1925—it was one of the last states to do so. Up until then, it had used a military flag.

Oregon City also became the seat of the US General Land Office (an agency in charge of public domain land)—the first federal land office west of the Rockies. Plats for the city of San Francisco, as well as Oregon City, were filed there. And Oregon City had **the only federal court on the West Coast** (established in 1848).

*Notable Historic Points*

In 1852, the seat of the Territorial government was moved to Salem. About that time, it began to construct plank roads from Portland south into the Willamette Valley. But at that time most supplies were moved along the valley by steamboats. The exception was at Jacksonville, where mule trains brought in miner's supplies from Crescent City.

## EARLY SHIPBUILDING IN OREGON

In the 1840s and 1850s, various types of ships began to be built in Oregon. The first keel-bottomed sailing ship to be built in Oregon was put together by Joseph Gale in 1841, and was launched on the Willamette River. It was called the *Star of Oregon*.

Beginning in the 1850s, steamboats began to be built in Oregon City and Milwaukie—examples include the *Hoosier*, the *Canemah*, and the *Lot Witcomb*. In 1851, steamboats began to move up and down the Willamette River. By 1878, fifty-two of them had been built in Oregon, mostly at a site just above Willamette Falls known as Canemah.

For the most part, the head of navigation on the Willamette was the city of Corvallis. For six months of the year, low water prevented most steamboats from reaching Eugene. The one exception was the *Canemah*, which was able to operate all year round on the upper river.

After 1874, two shallow-draft steamboats were constructed; these could make it to Eugene and then carry grain downriver to Portland. Constructed by Captain Uriah Scott, they were named the *Ohio* and the *City of Salem*.

Steamboats then also began moving along other rivers: the Columbia River between Portland and Astoria and upriver to The Dalles, and even the shallow Tualatin River. The *Columbia* was built in Astoria in 1850, the *Eliza Anderson* in Portland in 1858, and the *Novelty* at Clatskanie around 1878.[3]

The Oregon Steamship Navigation Company commenced service on the Columbia in 1860. Steamboats also plied Upper Klamath Lake and Goose Lake in eastern Oregon, providing easy transportation for residents.

[3] The first steamship to be operated on the Columbia River was the *Beaver*. Built in England, it was operated by the Hudson Bay Company in the mid-1830s.

**CHAPTER 2**

# DEVELOPMENT FIRSTS

In 1841, the Catholics established a school for boys in St. Paul; they established one for girls in 1844. The boys' school was the first school established in Oregon.

In 1842 in Salem, the Methodist Reverend Jason Lee started the second school in Oregon—the Oregon Institute—which in time became the **first institution of higher education in the West**. It is now known as Willamette University.

Some buildings from pioneer times are still standing. In Salem, they are the Jason Lee House and the Parsonage (thought to have been built before 1841, after Lee's arrival in 1834). They are the oldest surviving buildings in the Pacific Northwest (PNW).

Built in 1846, the home of Dr. John McLoughlin also still stands. Located in Oregon City, it is technically part of the Fort Vancouver National Historic Site (administered by the National Park Service). Another still-standing house in Oregon City dates to 1847—this is the William Holmes House, which was the site for the inauguration of the first governor of the Territory. Meetings of the Territorial legislature were held here. The first protestant church west of the Rockies (Methodist) was started in Oregon City in 1844.

In Eugene, the Lane County Clerk's building dates back to 1853. At Fort Dalles, the Surgeon's Quarters, built in 1857, still stands. So does the Guard

Oregon: A State That Stands Out

Ft. Dalles Surgeon's Quarters at The Dalles

4   From *The Great Northwest* (1960).

House at Fort Klamath—this building dates back to 1863.

The **first US post office on the West Coast** was in Astoria, beginning in 1847.

The **first US court session in the Pacific Northwest** took place at Lafayette, OR, in 1849.

The federal government built a Custom House in Astoria in 1852. This was the **first building west of the Rockies constructed by the federal government.** The first Customs Collector there was appointed in 1849.

In 1854, Wasco County was formed in all of what is now eastern Oregon, comprising what was then **the largest county ever formed in land that is now part of the contiguous United States**.

"Seldom on any frontier," wrote historian Oscar Osburn Winthur, in an appraisal of the settlers arriving on the Oregon Trail, "was there a more respectable…group of immigrants than those who comprised the membership of the great caravans that arrived annually over the Oregon Trail." Winthur contrasted these with the tough, boisterous types of retired mountain men, who also ended their years in Oregon. From the ranks of the respectable immigrants, Winthur said, "came the political, educational, and moral leadership" of the state.[4]

Oregon's constitution, drafted in 1857, incorporated a great deal of the constitution of the state of Indiana. Oregon became a state in 1859.

In 1856, the **first woolen mill on the West Coast** was started in Salem: the Willamette Woolen Manufacturing Company.

Four of Oregon's colleges were founded before statehood occurred: Willamette (1853, Methodist); Pacific (1854, Congregational), Linfield (1858, Baptist); and Columbia College in Eugene (1856, Presbyterian)—the latter lasted only four years, but it was among the **earliest co-educational colleges in the nation**. Lewis & Clark College started later (in 1868, Presbyterian) as the Albany Academy; it was eventually moved to Portland.

For over a century, Old College Hall at Pacific University (built in 1850) was **the oldest building used for higher education west of the Mississippi**. Nonetheless, Willamette University is the **oldest college in the PNW**.

The oldest secondary school in continuous operation in Oregon is St. Mary's Academy for girls in Portland—begun in 1859 by the Holy Names Sisters. Traveling 7000 miles from Montreal and sailing around Cape Horn, these women started the school two weeks after arriving. St. Mary's Academy continues to thrive, winning various awards and sending nearly all of its graduates to college.

Two years before St. Mary's founding, the first permanent school in the Northwest was started across the Columbia River in Vancouver —by Mother Joseph and the Providence Sisters. Later, in 1875, these sisters also started the Providence hospitals in Portland—the first permanent hospitals in Oregon.

Begun as a weekly in 1853, the *Oregonian* is the **oldest continuously operated newspaper west of Salt Lake City**. It was turned into a daily in 1861. The *Oregon Statesman* (in Salem) is the second oldest. The **earliest newspaper published in the West** was the *Oregon Spectator*, begun in 1846. It published mainly legal notices. But it was not a daily, and did not survive.

The **first photographic studio in the PNW** (and perhaps in the West) was in Jacksonville. It was opened in 1862 by Peter Britt.

The **first iron foundry west of the Rocky Mountains** opened in Lake Oswego in 1867 (using local hematite from Iron Mountain to produce pig iron). The Oregon Iron and Steel Company arose out of this operation, and remained in business until 1919.

Old College Hall at Pacific Unversity in Forest Grove

*Development Firsts*

Oregon: A State That Stands Out

Portland's Pioneer Courthouse (completed in 1875) is **the oldest in the PNW, and the second oldest west of the Mississippi River**. It is now a National Historic Landmark.

In the 1870s in Milwaukie, Seth Luelling **developed and introduced the Bing cherry**.

In 1879, Bethenia Owens of Roseburg became the **first woman doctor west of the Rockies**. She practiced in Portland for many years. Some have wondered whether the **first woman to vote in Oregon** might have been the stage driver who drove south from Jacksonville while disguised as the rugged one-eyed Charlie Parkhurst.

On December 17, 1887, a "golden spike" was driven at Ashland, connecting Oregon-built railroads with California-built railroads, and connecting Oregon's railroads with the national system. Afterwards, Oregon railroads became part of the Southern Pacific System.

The long-distance electrical transmission line from Willamette Falls to downtown Portland was **the nation's first high-tension electrical line**. Fourteen miles long, it went online on June 3, 1889. At first it used DC power; it was converted to AC in 1890.

The **first electric streetcars on the West Coast** were introduced in Portland in 1889.

The **first electric inter-urban trolley lines in the US** began in Oregon in 1893. The line ran to Portland from Oregon City. It continued until 1958—the **longest lifespan of any interurban railway in the US**. At first it was powered by steam, and then converted to electricity.

In 1889 Swiss Benedictine monks established Mount Angel Abbey, which was the **first Catholic Seminary in the West to educate candidates for the priesthood**.

In 1893, Marylhurst College in Lake Oswego was **the PNW's first liberal arts college for women**. Still in operation, it is also Oregon's oldest Catholic college, set up by the Sisters of the Holy Names.

Iron Furnace at Lake Oswego

16 | CHAPTER 2

The **oldest library west of the Mississippi River** (now known as the Multnomah County Library) opened in Portland in 1864, beginning as a private library and then becoming a public one in 1902.

**Cloud Cap Inn,** built in 1889 on the northeast side of Mt. Hood (at an elevation of 6000 feet), is **the oldest alpine inn in the West**. Financed by C. E. S. Wood and banker William Ladd, it functioned for a while as a full-service mountain inn. But after years of rough winter weather, it had begun to show signs of wear. The "Crag Rats" of Hood River (a mountain rescue group) has led the way in restoring it.

The **oldest federal wildlife refuge in the West** is at Three Arch Rocks on the Oregon Coast near Tillamook. The refuge was set aside in 1907 by President Theodore Roosevelt, at the behest of Oregon's William L. Finley.

In 1908, the Klamath National Wildlife Refuge was the **first large area of public land set aside for that purpose**. Eighty percent of the waterfowl flying along the Pacific Coast Flyway stop there—once as many as six million of them.

Old Federal Courthouse in Portland

# CHAPTER 3
# RECORD-SETTING FEATURES

Oregon has also set records in various unusual ways.

**One of the largest lilac bushes anywhere** now grows outside of the Philip Foster farm in Eagle Creek (20 miles east of Portland). It was brought from Calais, Maine, by pioneer Mary Foster, and was planted here in 1847. An old-fashioned variety of lilac, it has a heavy fragrance and has achieved a staggering size. The farm is on the National Register of Historic Places. It was part of an effort to soften the new homes of pioneers on the frontier.

Oregon has **fifty-six ghost towns—more than any other state**. Consider, for instance, the one-time gold mining town of Cornucopia, south of the Wallowas. Established in the 1880s, the Cornucopia mine produced over $10 million worth of gold until it expired in 1941. The buildings there still stand, but the residents are all gone. Another former town—Kinzua, in Wheeler County—has not even survived as a ghost town. Once a lumber company town, it was demolished and the site planted over with trees.

Among western states, **Oregon has the most covered bridges** (fifty-one). Most are west of the Cascades, in rainy country, and were built in the 1920s and 30s. The longest one is in Westfir. It is 180 feet long. It is also the tallest covered bridge west of the Mississippi River. Of the 500 that once did exist, only 48 remain. Many of them are on the National Register.

18 | Oregon: A State That Stands Out

Goodpasture Covered Bridge near Vida

The Happy Canyon Indian Pageant, near Pendleton, is the **longest running outdoor pageant and Wild West show** in the nation. Half the participants are Indians. It has been running since 1914.

The Warm Springs Reservation is **one of the few whose size has not decreased over time**, through allotments or otherwise. It belongs to the Confederated Tribes of Warm Springs.

In 1864, **the largest woolen mill west of the Mississippi River was at Oregon City**. It laid the foundation for the important woolen industry that emerged in the state.

*Record-Setting Features*

Gold was once found at Whiskey Run, in the sands of its beach placers—about a half dozen miles north of the mouth of the Coquille River. It was an unusual site for a mine.

The multiple-lift locks around Willamette Falls—built by the Corps of Engineers in 1873—are the **oldest in the nation**.

Oregon once had a steamboat that strove to offer the elegance of a Mississippi River boat. This was the *Oneonta*, a side-wheel steamboat that operated in the 1860s on the Columbia River, upstream from the Cascades. It was operated by the Oregon Steam Navigation Company.

In 1874, a very fast clipper ship—known as both the ***Western Shore*** and the ***Oregon Clipper***—was built in Oregon at North Bend by Captain Asa Simpson and his brother. The ship **soon set records for the speed of its trips to England**. However, before long a drunken skipper wrecked it on Duxbury Reef, while approaching San Francisco.

Oneonta Sternwheeler

The unique Round Barn, built by rancher Peter French near Malheur Lake, is listed on the National Register. Built in the 1880s, it was a kind of enclosed corral, built of peeled Juniper poles. At one time, French had a ranch of over 150,000 acres in the region. Another remnant of French's era can be seen in Frenchglen, a small hotel now on the National Register and owned by the state park department.

Since it was founded in 1880, a boarding school for Indians has been in continuous operation just north of Salem: the **Chemawa Indian School**. It is the **oldest such school**. Not all agree that such schools have had a positive effect.

In the 1880s, **Portland's Central School** was thought by some to have been **the largest public-school building west of the Mississippi River**.

The lighthouse built on **Tillamook Rock** in 1881 was then the **most expensive lighthouse ever built** in the United States. It was originally planned for Tillamook Head—but soon it was discovered that this location is often shrouded in fog, and thus unsuitable.

Tillamook Rock was a little more than a mile offshore, but was a very difficult site on which to build. In trying to reach the one-acre rock, the initial surveyor was swept to his death. Once the lighthouse was built, it turned out to be too expensive to operate (in fact, it held the record for operating costs). The lighthouse was often hit by huge waves and punishing storms; it was hard to get lighthouse keepers on and off it. Repairs were constantly needed. Nicknamed "Terrible Tilly," it was shut down in 1957. It is now mute testimony to an unfortunate mistake.

Frenchglen Hotel

Another Oregon lighthouse holds the record for **shortest period of operation**: the small **Yaquina Bay Lighthouse**, which lasted only three years, from 1871 to 1874. It was found that the one nearby, on Yaquina Head, could do the job better.

The lighthouse with the happiest record is the **Heceta Head Lighthouse** (built in 1894)—located to the south, in Lane County. Because it is so scenic, it is the **most photographed lighthouse on the Pacific Coast**. It is operates with a fine Fresnel lens—now a rarity.

The **Wolf Creek Tavern** (twenty miles north of Grants Pass) is the **oldest continuously operating inn** in the Northwest. It was established in 1883, and became a popular stopping point on the stage coach route between Redding and Roseburg. Later, it attracted movie greats such as Clark Gable, Carole Lombard, Orson Welles, Mary Pickford, and Douglas Fairbanks—as well as author Jack London. In the 1970s, the state acquired it, and it has since been run by the parks department.

Wolf Creek Tavern

*Record-Setting Features*

Oregon: A State That Stands Out

Forestry Center (world's largest log cabin) at 1905 Lewis and Clark Exposition

Astoria Column

Oregon's **Pendleton Round-Up** is **one of the top ten rodeos on the continent;** some even argue it is one of the best in the world. It is known for combining cowboy culture with a celebration of Indian culture; many champions appear in its events. It began in 1910.

The **world's largest log cabin** was in Portland—the **Forestry Building**, built in 1905 for the Lewis and Clark Exposition. It was designed by A. E. Doyle and was seventy-two feet tall. It was destroyed in a 1964 fire caused by faulty wiring.

Portland's **Lewis and Clark Exposition** (1905) was **one of the few World's Fairs at which suffragists were permitted to appear**. As these activists unveiled a statue of Sacajawea, Susan B. Anthony spoke of the importance of this Indian woman who had led American explorers here. This was also one of the few World's Fairs that actually made a profit. The grounds were laid out by famous landscape architect John Charles Olmstead, and reflected the ideals of the City Beautiful movement.

In 1913, Portland had **the third most extensive electric railway system in America**; Portland called it the "World's Finest Trolley System." There were 600 streetcars on 273 miles of lines. In the first years of the twentieth century, it even had cable-operated street cars of the San Francisco type.

St. Johns Bridge in Portland

Owyhee Dam

At one time, over twenty percent of the streets of Portland were lined with rose hedges. This practice began in 1902, in anticipation of the Lewis and Clark Exposition. The city even distributed free cuttings (of the "Madame Caroline Testout" variety) to those who promised to plant them.

Located in Harney County, the **Crane Union High School** is the **oldest public boarding school** in the country—it was established in 1923. It boards children of families living on remote ranches.

The **Astor Column in Astoria** was built in 1926 by the Great Northern Railroad to celebrate the westward expansion of the United States. At 125 feet, it is **one of the tallest memorial columns in the West** and was modeled on Trajan's Column in Rome. Much of its funding was provided by Vincent Astor, a grandson of John Jacob Astor. A painted mural of the history of Astoria spirals up it. It was restored in 1995 and has been added to the National Register of Historic Places.

When the Jantzen Beach Amusement Park was opened in north Portland in 1928, its **Big Dipper** was **the largest roller coaster west of Chicago**. The Park was called the "Wonder of the West."

When it was constructed over the Willamette River in 1931, Portland's **St. John's Bridge** was the **largest suspension bridge in the world**. At that time, it

*Record-Setting Features*

had a record amount of clearance under its center span, as well as the tallest reinforced concrete piers (at 183 feet). While newer bridges now exceed those records, the bridge is still celebrated for its elegance. It was the favorite of one of its designers, David B. Steinman.

When it was constructed in 1932, eastern Oregon's 417-foot-tall **Owyhee Dam** was the **highest arch-gravity dam in the world**. It was even used by the Bureau of Reclamation as the prototype for Hoover Dam. But a few years later, higher dams were erected.

**Timberline Lodge** on Mt. Hood is the **only major park-like resort built and owned by the federal government.** It was built by the WPA in 1936 for the US Forest Service. (In most national parks, the private concessionaires who finance the lodges have a "possessory interest"—similar to a lease—in these structures.) A number of WPA-era murals decorate the interior of the lodge. (Such murals can also be found in a number of Oregon post offices, such as in Eugene, Burns, and Ontario; most tell the story of settlement.)

The nearby **Silcox Hut**, at nearly 7000 feet and at the edge of the Palmer Snowfield, is **one of the most elaborate permanent rustic lodges at that elevation**. It has overnight facilities for twenty-four people, and provides meals. Sno-cats take visitors to the hut. It is probably one of the highest such lodges on the West Coast.

When **Bonneville Dam** was finished in 1938, it provided a huge amount of electric power for the Northwest (through the lines of the Bonneville Power Administration). That system provided the energy **used to produce aluminum for a third of the aircraft built in World War II**, as well as for the development of the atomic bomb at Hanford, WA. With numerous power plants, **the Columbia River Basin produces more hydroelectric power than anywhere else in the United States**.

At the time it was built, **Bonneville Dam** had the **largest single-lift lock in the world**. Now the John Day Dam has **the highest single-lift locks in the western hemisphere**.

Of the dozen **Oregon coast bridges** designed by state engineer Conde McCullough, eleven survive. Now viewed as "coastal jewels," bridge specialists have said they "represent what may be the finest continuous set of concrete-reinforced, steel-arched bridges in the United States." In fact, others have said these are "some of the best and most innovative concrete and steel bridge designs in the world."

Others, characterizing them as "**masterpieces in design**," have said they are valued so highly because of the way they combine exceptional architectural design with engineering advances, and are fitted into their natural setting. McCullough is now seen as "one of the nation's most accomplished bridge designers."

State engineers have taken the initiative to place these bridges on the National Register of Historic Places. Renovation plans are underway, so as to avoid tearing any more of them down (unfortunately, one has already met that fate).

McCullough's bridges were built in the 1930s, during the Depression, and the WPA financed them at a cost of $5.4 million. Some he designed were built

Yaquina Bay Bridge (McCullough Bridge) at Newport

elsewhere in the state; for instance, see the arch bridge between Oregon City and West Linn, which was refurbished in 2012.

The **oldest footwear in the world** was discovered in 1938 in eastern Oregon (near Fort Rock) by University of Oregon (U of O) anthropologist Luther Cressman. It consisted of 10,000 year-old sandals made of sagebrush, which had been covered by volcanic ash from the eruption of Mt. Mazama.

Now **a small orange agate tool** has been found in southeastern Oregon at the Rimrock Draw Rockshelter that may be **even older than the rock tools found in Clovis, New Mexico** (which had been thought to be the oldest cultural artifacts in the Americas). This Oregon tool was found under a layer of ash from an explosion of Mt. St. Helens that occurred 15,800 years ago.

One of the **oldest sites showing continuing human occupancy over a long period** is the Five-Mile Rapids site in Wasco County. Humans lived here from the end of the glacial period—between 9000 BCE and 1820 CE. A place where the densest concentrations of natives lived is on Sauvie Island. This Chinookian village was occupied between the thirteenth and eighteenth centuries, CE.

Oregon is **one the few states whose capitol building departs from the style of classical architecture**. It is one of only three states having a capitol building in art-deco style; its is the most distinctive. Built in 1938 after the earlier one burned, and financed in part by the WPA, it has since been both doubled in size and renovated. It was the first state capitol to produce power by installing photovoltaic panels.

The world's **largest wooden building** is found at Tillamook, Oregon. Its claim is based on the fact that its clear span is not matched by any other structure. The US Navy built two such buildings in Tillamook during World War II as **hangers for blimps** that patrolled this part of the Pacific coast, searching for enemy submarines. The one that remains is a fifth of a mile in length and twenty-one stories high.

The **Steamboat Inn,** on the North Fork of the Umpqua River, caters to anglers who come to fish America's "**most revered steelhead stream**" (as Jack Hemmingway put it). The current inn was established in 1957, but an earlier version existed in the 1930s. Guide Frank Moore built it, and it is now celebrated as Oregon's most famous fishing lodge. It is regarded as **one of the finest country inns** on the West Coast.

When the **Pacific Gas and Electric's dam on the North Fork of the Clackamas River** was relicensed in 1958, it was required to add a remarkably long fish ladder. At that time, it was the **highest fish ladder in the world (and one of the longest)**. The ladder runs for two miles, and the pipe, designed to carry small fish downstream, runs for five miles.

Oregon produced the **only geared locomotive in the US** to deal with its steep slopes.

**The Astoria-Megler Bridge** (which crosses the Columbia River) is listed by *Guinness World Records* as the **longest bridge with three spans and continuous through-trusses**.

Most windstorms of hurricane strength strike the Gulf Coast states. But Oregon's **Columbus Day Storm** of October 12, 1962 **had the strength of a tropical storm**, reaching wind speeds of 145 mph as it hit Cape Blanco. Over half the storm's fatalities were in Oregon, and it flattened huge amounts of standing timber.

In the period of 1940-1949, Oregon grew by 59.3 percent—the **fastest growth rate in the country**, and a result of a wartime economy.

The **Wallowa Lake Tramway**, rising 3700 feet to Mt. Howard (elevation 8150 feet), is the **steepest four-person gondola in North America**. It was built in 1968 and overlooks

Blimp Hangar at Tillamook

*Record-Setting Features*

Wallowa Lake (a glacial "finger lake"). Nearby, an abandoned railroad track that runs from Elgin to Joseph now has America's only pedal-powered cart operating on it.

The **Siletz Indian Reservation** was among **a very few to be terminated (in 1955) and then restored to federal recognition (in 1977)**. It was only the second to follow this course.

Monmouth, Oregon holds the US record as **the town banning the sale of alcohol for the longest period of time**: from the mid-nineteenth century until 2002. Monmouth residents with a thirst for alcohol could get it at the nearby town of Independence during this time.

## CHAPTER 4

# THINGS THAT GIVE OREGON CHARACTER

Oregon has acquired interest and character by virtue of various things that have happened in the state.

In 1837, a new settler, Ewing Young, ventured to California to obtain a herd of 630 black Spanish longhorn cattle, which he and his associates then drove back to the Willamette Valley. But these cattle soon became wild and, growing in numbers, soon changed the valley's ecology with their grazing habits. **This was the first cattle drive in the West.**

When the explorer John C. Fremont traveled in 1843 through the forests of Ponderosa pine near today's Bend, he exulted over the trees' beauty and uniform size. A decade later, when the surveyors for the Pacific Railroad Survey moved through this same area, they remarked on how open (i.e., widely-spaced) they were. Alas, today few of these fine forests remain.

In 1845, two Portland settlers competed to see which one of their home towns the as-of-yet unnamed area would be named after: Portland, Maine or Boston, Massachusetts. In three tosses of a coin, Francis Pettygrove (hailing from the former city) won. The coin that they used is on display in the Oregon Historical Society Museum in Portland.

Many pioneer women sought flowers to brighten the yards of their new homes. At French Prairie and the Methodist Mission near Salem, they were given rootstocks of a pink rose that would soon be called the "Mission Rose."

Michael McCloskey | 29

At Fort Vancouver, this would become a local tradition for new brides. It is not known whether the roses were brought from England, New England (by the bride of missionary Jason Lee), or the California Missions.

Miners disembarked from steamboats at The Dalles in the late 1860s and made their way overland to the new mines near Baker City. Some twenty-two saloons, gambling houses, and bordellos helped them on their way. Tons of freight too were unloaded there for them.

In 1866, the Oregon Stage Lines advertised that its stages ran from Portland to Sacramento in six days. Henry W. Corbett started the lines, having secured the contract to carry mail. He was soon to become a US Senator, but before then, Portland's stage lines were connected with Salt Lake City and St. Louis via the stage lines run by the Wells Fargo firm.

In 1877, the US Army and settlers tried to drive a band of the Nez Perce tribe out of their homeland in the Wallowa Valley in eastern Oregon; the tribe had refused to sign a treaty. As they resisted, hostilities developed and a war broke out, ending eventually in the surrender of the retreating tribe in Montana. For months, the Nez Perce had outmaneuvered the US Army. Their chief, Joseph, then proclaimed: "From where the sun now stands, I will fight no more forever." A young lieutenant, C.E.S. Wood, recorded his words. Amazingly, they later became friends.

It is hard to believe that the last of the Oregon Indian Wars were still going on in the late 1870s, when new settlers were building steamboats, railroads, and cities in the state.

Oregon ports were the scene of "shanghaiing" as a way to muster crews for sailing vessels during the late nineteenth and early twentieth century. During the transition from sailing to steam-powered vessels, the former faced increasing difficulties keeping crews. Forcible recruitment was one solution. This happened in ports such as Coos Bay, Astoria, and even Portland.

In the 1880s, Portland liked to claim that it had **the longest bar in the world**: all 684 feet of it running the length of a block on both sides of a building on lower Burnside. This was Erickson's, which also was proud to call itself the "grandest and rowdiest workingman's bar in the country." Loggers, miners, and sailors crowded in to quench their thirst, as well as to get a legendary free lunch, complemented by non-stop gambling and entertainment. The original bar lasted until 1912, when it was destroyed in a fire.

When the Northern Pacific Railroad reached Portland in 1883, "lavish decorations, pageants, and parades" greeted it. In fact, along First Street, three temporary triumphal arches were erected to welcome the railroad—from Stark to Ankeny. At the time, city fathers thought Portland was about to become a great new metropolis.

In the 1890s, Oregon had an eccentric Populist governor: Sylvester Pennoyer. He was noted for such tart comments as: "No permission will be given to use a state cannon for firing a salute over the inauguration of a Wall Street plutocrat as President of the United States"; Democratic legislators had made that request for the 1892 inauguration of Grover Cleveland. When that President later asked the governor to take due precautions to prevent violence regarding a controversial law, Pennoyer replied: "I will attend to my business; let the president attend to his."

Since the 1890s, mail has been delivered along the lower Rogue River by mail boats. They still run the sixty-four miles from Gold Beach up to Agness and back on most days.

The US battleship *Oregon*, built in San Francisco in 1896, was the first modern battleship in Pacific waters. On the eve of the Spanish-American War, the *Oregon* made the trip around the Horn in record time, firing the first shots in the Battle of Santiago. In World War I, it was the flagship of the Pacific Fleet and escorted troopships to Siberia. On retirement, it spent a number of years as a floating memorial in Portland, and its mast is now preserved as a memorial in Tom McCall Waterfront Park.

In 1900, the Oregon Historical Society took the lead in restoring the site of a salt works established by members of the Lewis and Clark expedition in what is now Seaside. In the winter of 1805, five men had spent two months boiling seawater there to make salt for curing meat. The site can now be seen on the southern end of Seaside, off South Promenade on Lewis and Clark Way.

Noted impressionist painter Childe Hassam came to Oregon to paint twice: in 1904 and 1908. He was invited by C.E.S. Wood, who had retired from the Army, and had become an influential Oregon attorney. As Wood had taken up painting too, they painted together, particularly in the Harney Desert. The Portland Art Museum displays a number of their paintings from these trips. Wood was one of the founders of the Museum.

In the first few years of the twentieth century, range wars broke out in eastern Oregon's ranges and forests. Battles took place between sheep herders and cattlemen, and also between sheep herders and those bringing sheep in from California. As many as 10,000 sheep were shot. Homes were burned, timber stolen, and illegal fences thrown up. The violence led to these areas being set aside by the federal government as Forest Reserves (these are the areas now known as the Umatilla and Ochoco National Forests).

In the 1880s, patent medicines were common, but few were enveloped in as much hokum as one then claiming connections to Oregon. It was supposedly produced by the Oregon Indian Medicine Company, and made of herbs collected by Indians on the Warm Springs and Nez Perce reservations. It was called the Ka-Ton-Ka tonic and was supposed to cure headaches, liver disorders, and female complaints. It was really a combination of alcohol, sugar, aloes, and baking soda. And it was the product of the fertile imagination of the supposed "Colonel," T.A. Edwards, who had merely passed through the state. Its production was finally stopped in 1905 due to charges of false advertising.

Oregon was long beset by the race problems at the bottom of the Civil War. For a long time, the state had trouble in the way it dealt with slavery and blacks. In deciding what provisions to put into the Oregon constitution (written in 1859), its voters decided that slavery could not be established in the state. Though this might be seen as a victory for the Union side, it merely continued a provision that Congress adopted in authorizing the Oregon territory in 1848. Oregon voters also specified that free blacks could not live in the state. Though this might be seen as a victory for the Southern side, it merely continued a position embodied in territorial legislation adopted in 1849.

For a century (1850-1950), Oregon did not seem to care whether its conduct fit its official policies. Oregonian blacks were supposed to have been whipped twice a year; under the state's constitution, blacks could not in theory vote; and interracial marriage was not supposedly permitted. And Oregon would not ratify the fifteenth amendment (giving African-American men the right to vote). This was all a result of southern sentiment transferred to Oregon, as many early settlers came from the South.

But all of this was just political posturing. Blacks did live in the state; while some were brought here as slaves, there was a territorial supreme court decision against slavery as early as 1853; there were 128 blacks in Oregon when it became a state; blacks here were not whipped; no practical obstacles were raised to interracial marriage.

And some evidence of improving prospects for blacks began to be seen. The first black policeman was hired in Portland in 1904. There was a branch of the NAACP in Portland by the second decade of the twentieth century—it is the oldest west of the Mississippi. In the 1920s, blacks in Portland found ways to buy homes, even though laws supposedly disallowing black homeownership were on the books and were not repealed until 1926. A black woman was admitted to the Oregon bar in 1922.

Practically speaking, it did not matter that the state did not ratify the fifteenth amendment; it was already in effect by virtue of federal action, and federal law was controlling. After the Civil War, the legal right to vote by men of all races in Oregon was not a problem.

And until they came into the state in World War II to work in the state's shipyards, there were few blacks here to complain about the state's curious racial laws. (Indeed, they may not have felt welcome up to that time.) For the most part, the situation was the product of the history of southerners migrating to Oregon. Eventually, most of these theoretical problems got resolved. However, blacks continued to be the object of discrimination, as they did in most of the country.

Hostility against Chinese workers in the state was not theoretical. The worst outbreak came in 1887, at Deep Creek in Hells Canyon, when thirty-one Chinese miners were killed over two days in a robbery that took $50,000 of their gold. While it is now thought that the perpetrators were local white ranchers, no one was ever convicted. New scholarship suggests the county government suppressed critical evidence. One scholar considers this the worst incident of anti-Chinese violence in the American West. He said "its brutality was unexcelled." At that time, Chinese workers constituted nearly six percent of the state's population.

For fifty years (beginning in the 1890s), Oregon was taken with the idea of Chautauqua events—a cultural phenomenon in the late nineteenth century and early twentieth century that emphasized adult education and cultural improvement—with major events held in Ashland, Gladstone, Corvallis, and La Grande. Imposing structures were often erected to house these programs. The principal booking agent on the West Coast was in Portland: the Ellison-White Chautauqua System.

In the period of 1888-1897, Oregon in effect had a Populist governor: Sylvester Pennoyer. Though elected as a Democrat, he later switched to the new Populist Party. In 1889, at a convention in Salem, delegates from the Grange, various labor unions, and prohibitionists formed the Populist Party of Oregon. In the preceding decade, as many as 181 local Granges had been formed in Oregon. The Populists denounced "the power of the trusts and corporations" and "the land-grabbers of the public domain." They were influential in the period of 1892-1896.

While the Republicans reclaimed the governorship in 1897, they lost it again to Democrat George Chamberlain in 1902. He was re-elected four years later and then followed by one-term Democrat Oswald West. It can hardly be said that the Republicans had a lock on the governorship after the 1880s. In the twenty-eight years between 1888 and 1916, Democrats had the governorship for twenty.

In the first decade of the twentieth century, Oregon was convulsed by federal trials of many of its top officials. They were being prosecuted for perpetrating fraudulent claims for federal lands and because of their cover-ups. C.E.S. Wood had denounced "the thieves that have been carrying off valuable lands." President Theodore Roosevelt sent investigators and lawyers out to clean up the mess. 126 convictions were obtained. All of those convicted were fellow Republicans; some Democratic officials, such as Oswald West, fought the frauds.

Portland has fifty-two of **the nation's most iconic and distinctive public drinking fountains**. These are the so-called "Benson Bubblers," built in 1912 with a donation from Simon Benson. With four arms in Greek style (each with a small fountain), they provide fresh water for the thirsty throughout the year. They were designed by A.E. Doyle.

Benson Bubbler in Portland

The Willamette River is still crossed by three ferries: the Wheatland and Buena Vista ferries (both in Marion county), and the Canby ferry. On the lower Columbia River, a ferry still goes from Westport out to Puget Island.

Only a few states still have "millraces." In the heyday of industrialization, these races (or channels) diverted flows of water from nearby rivers to run downstream through towns, powering mills for various purposes, such as for grinding flour. Oregon still has remnants of them in two of its cities, Salem and Eugene. While at times the millraces have been damaged by floods, they have sentimental and historic value for these cities, and have been continuously restored. The oldest surviving water-powered mill for grinding flour is Thompson's Mill in Shedd (south of Albany).

## ODDS AND ENDS

In 1903 Portland's Oaks Park, once accessible by streetcars, was labeled the "Coney Island of the West."

In 1912, a stunt pilot flew a plane off the roof of Portland's Multnomah Hotel. Oregon City has the only municipal outdoor elevator in the nation.

In the first decade of the twentieth century, Klamath County was beset by disputes over which of three county courthouses it should claim. For a while, the bets were on a stately new courthouse with Greek columns on all sides. But after litigation raged over every option, the one with columns was found to be unsound. It was demolished before it could be used. Perhaps the casual ranchers of the Klamath Falls area found it to be too formal.

In 1910, two incompetent pirates tried to take over a passenger steamship as it was cruising by the mouth of the Umpqua River. Their aim was to steal three tons of Yukon gold on its way to San Francisco, and then run the steamer ashore. But they were unprepared to deal with resistant passengers, who turned out to be armed. The crew also fought back. The pirates also had no way to carry away that much heavy gold, and one of them jumped overboard. After hiding, the other soon lost his mind.

**The last of the railroad wars occurred along Oregon's Deschutes River** between 1908 and 1912. On the east and west sides of the river, two railroad magnates competed to build railroads. E.H. Harriman of the Union Pacific (through a subsidiary) worked to build a railroad on the east bank, while James J. Hill, through a subsidiary (the Spokane, Portland, and Seattle Railway) worked to build a railway along the west bank. Those involved resorted to land grabs, intimidation, vandalism, arson, and even murder. By 1912, the competing railroads were completed. They operated separately for some time, before finally being consolidated.

In 1906 Harriman acquired property on the west bank of Upper Klamath Lake on Pelican Bay; he called it the Harriman Springs Lodge. Summertime guests included the naturalist John Muir, who was a friend of Harriman's.

When the railroad finally reached Bend in 1911, it bypassed Prineville. Desperate that no railroad would connect it with the main line, Prineville finally decided to start its own: the City of Prineville Railway, running all of nineteen miles toward Redmond. While its early years were not encouraging, in due course the railroad became very profitable, as major mills came to town and used it to ship their lumber. In fact, when that happened, the city even stopped levying local taxes. What a wonderful business decision!

Bill Hanley, of Burns, was a jumble of contradictions. He was a wealthy rancher, conservationist, progressive politician, and railroad promoter. Given these interests, he was a friend of William Jennings Bryan, Theodore Roosevelt, C.E.S. Wood, and Will Rogers. Hanley and C.E.S. Wood both collaborated on projects with railroader James J. Hill.

Born in Jacksonville in 1861, Hanley became one of the largest ranchers in eastern Oregon. Eventually, parts of his ranch holdings became part of the Malheur National Wildlife Refuge. He reveled in the millions of migratory birds that visited his ranchlands. Sometimes he even fed them.

He ran unsuccessful populist campaigns for a US Senate seat from Oregon, and for the state's governorship. He did well in Harney County and Portland. It seems his progressive, conservation-oriented views did not keep him from becoming a successful rancher. He controlled over 200,000 acres and took care of his lands.

In 1911, an Oregon forester (William Bushnell Osborne) invented the key instrument used in forest fire lookouts: the fire finder.

The flamboyant Socialist candidate for the Presidency, Eugene V. Debs, drew ten percent of Oregon's vote in the 1912 election.

In 1913, reformers in Portland replaced its city council— fifteen members elected by wards—with four full-time commissioners and a mayor, all elected at large. It was hoped that the new system would be more professional and less partisan. However, today many feel it is an anachronism; it is the only city with this system.

Basque sheep herders in Jordan Valley built a walled field in 1915 to play the (relatively rare, in this country) game of pelota fronton; the field can still be seen there today.

In those days, when the Basques tending sheep on the west slope of Steens Mountain felt lonely, they got solace from "women of the night," who stayed in wagons there at a spot surrounded by aspens, later called "Whorehouse Meadow." It is still noted on detailed maps of the area.

Virgil Earp, the brother of famed western sheriff Wyatt Earp, is buried in Portland's Riverview Cemetery.

Oregon is **one of the few states in which a major block of land (2.8 million acres), which had passed into private ownership, was taken back ("re-vested") into public ownership**. The land had been granted to the Oregon and California Railroad for building a railroad line between points in the two states. However, the railroad was not completed on time, nor were the grant lands sold to farmers (as required). Not only were the terms of the grant not met—massive fraud occurred as well. The Chamberlain-Ferris Act (1916) returned these lands to the federal government (i.e., put in the care of the Interior Department).

In the winter of 1913-14, Oregon Governor Oswald West imposed martial law on a mining village along the Snake River in eastern Baker County. He had received a petition from a majority of its citizens, claiming that state laws were being flouted—and more specifically, that the saloons never closed, that they allowed gambling, and that alcohol was served on Sundays. In response, he sent in a contingent of militia who seized the gambling equipment, the liquor, and the weapons, and then closed the saloons. All of the town's city officials were arrested. This precipitated a contest in the courts over the legality of his action. When the case went to the State Supreme Court, that court upheld the governor's action. This was known as the Copperfield Affair. The saloons never reopened, and the town soon burned.

During World War I, the US Army took control of all logging operations in the woods of Oregon (and other Northwest states). This was because it feared that the radical IWW (Industrial Workers of the World, also known as the "Wobblies"), which opposed the war, was going to stir up unrest in the woods.

That union was then strong in logging operations and was thought to be planning a massive strike. Spruce was being logged for light aircraft for the army air corps. A compulsory paramilitary union (the Loyal Legion of Loggers and Lumbermen), sponsored by management, took over. The "Wobblies" never recovered. The Army also took over various spruce mills, including ones in Toledo and Coquille (under the government's Spruce Production Board).

In the first part of the 1920s (a time of ferment), the Ku Klux Klan attracted over two million supporters across the country. Some of them were in Oregon, responding to organizers who came here from the South.

If there had been many blacks here then, the Klan would have aroused ill-feeling toward them. Instead, they made Catholics the object of their animus. In 1922, the Klan pushed an initiative that would have put Oregon parochial schools out of business. But though the initiative passed, it was challenged by a society of teaching sisters who, in 1925, got it overturned by both the US and Oregon Supreme Court. On the other hand, the KKK did get some Catholic public school teachers fired.

From the beginning, the Oregon KKK was wracked by internal strife over the dictatorial methods of its leaders. For a few years, its political machine enjoyed some success, but it soon faded from the scene. The KKK was opposed throughout the state by many newspapers and leaders such as Governor Ben Olcott. While in 1923 the KKK claimed to control the legislature, it could not pass most of its program; and while it claimed that it had elected Walter Pierce as governor, in due course Pierce distanced himself from the group.

In the 1920s, a radio program was broadcast nationally, promoting Oregon. Written and performed by Frank Branch Riley of Portland, it was labeled the "Lure of the Great Northwest."

In the period between 1915 and 1933, competing interurban electric railways ran up and down the Willamette Valley. The "green ones" were run by the Oregon Electric Railway, and the "red ones" by the Southern Pacific Railroad.

*Things That Give Oregon Character*

In the 1920s and 30s, descendants of Oregon pioneers started a tradition of putting on celebrations and reenactments of pioneer times. The greatest of these events was in Eugene, where between 1926 and 1950, pioneer descendants mounted a grand re-enactment of the trek westward. Calling this the Pioneer Pageant, they reached out to all parts of the state to invite people to join in. Many did. Thousands of Eugene residents worked together to mount these events.

Wearing beards and pioneer costumes, the re-enactors marched with oxen, "prairie schooners," and "big wheels" (used to transport big logs). They were usually led by Cal Young, one of the first people born of pioneer stock in the new state. The event culminated in a program of music, dance, poetry, and tableaux. And every three to five years, they did it again.

By all accounts, the ones in 1929, 1934, and 1937 were the most memorable. But gradually, as the people of that generation passed from the scene, and pioneer relics became scarce, interest in these pageants waned. But these spectacles, and the enthusiasm they engendered, are still remembered. They too are a final part of the era of the pioneers.

The 1932 march of World War I veterans upon Washington, D.C. began in Portland, Oregon. Known as the "Bonus Army," unemployed veterans resolved to march upon Washington to present a petition to the federal government—asking it to pay their enlistment bonus early, since their need then was so urgent, as this was during the Depression. Because Portland veterans were especially vocal, veterans along the West Coast gathered in that city to travel east. In due course, great numbers assembled in Washington, D.C., but got no response. Eventually the Army used force to

Bonus Army of 1932 in Portland

disperse them. That dispersal prompted resentment, generating adverse publicity that helped shape the politics of the next Presidential election. An Oregon native, Walter W. Waters, was the veterans' outspoken leader.

A similar effort was made thirty years earlier (Coxey's Army, 1893), when unemployed workers tried to march on Washington in a bid for aid during an earlier time of economic distress. When hundreds gathered in Portland to try to commandeer rail cars, President Cleveland ordered the US Army to drive them off. When he asked Oregon governor Sylvester Pennoyer to have his militia help, Pennoyer refused, replying: "Let Cleveland's army take care of Coxey's army." Pennoyer later supported Coxey's Army in a speech made in downtown Portland before an audience of cheering thousands.

Bend Water Pageant (Historic)

In the 1920s, Portland opened its first airport, on Swan Island. In 1932, it was called "**the most beautiful airport in the nation**."

The inventor of the Gilbert Chemistry Set and the Erector Set hailed from Salem, and his works can be seen at a museum there: The Gilbert House Children's Museum.

**The world's largest private athletic club** is **Portland's Multnomah Athletic Club**, which has 20,000 members.

At one time, elaborate floats paraded at night along watercourses in some Oregon towns, creating a magical effect with their lights. Beginning in 1915, students at the University of Oregon used to do this along the millrace for homecoming, calling the practice the "canoe fete." Over time, the canoe fete began to involve a procession of highly decorated floats. The annual event became very popular, attracting crowds. It reached its peak in 1935, when it was covered nationally in newsreels. Bing Crosby even offered a prize for the best float. Eventually it all got to be too expensive, however. It ended in 1971.

In 1933, with the Eugene pageants still fresh in their minds, U of O graduates started a similar event in Bend, on Drake Pond. Calling it their Water Pageant, it also attracted crowds of thousands. In 1960, the celebration lasted for three days, with that year's Miss America the headliner. But by 1965, the Water Pageant too had become too expensive and unwieldy, and was brought to close.

But both created romantic diversions that few who saw them ever forgot.

In the Depression years, the political patterns in Oregon began to change. The long-standing dominance of the Republican Party, which had emerged in the 1880s, started to give way. In 1930, Julius Meier was elected governor; he was an Independent who favored public power. In the presidential election, Democrat Franklin Roosevelt then captured Oregon's vote, and kept doing it (getting as much as 68 percent of the vote in 1936).

In 1934, another Democrat named Charles Martin, who claimed he supported the New Deal, was elected governor. Long-time Republican US Senator, Charles McNary, also supported the New Deal, as well as consolidating his standing as a leading progressive on the West Coast. When Charles Martin began to stray from being a New Dealer, Charles Sprague was put in his place; while nominally a Republican, Sprague was really a very independent progressive.

The Democrats also captured the state House of Representatives during these times. This newfound success did not last, but the foundations of Oregon politics had been shaken. By the 1950s, the Democrats had replaced the Republicans as Oregon's dominant party.

During the Great Depression, citizens of North Bend (near Coos Bay) used scraps of Myrtlewood as scrip in place of money when the city's only bank closed and money became scarce. Amazingly, this scrip can still be redeemed today.

In the same period, Oregon was a major location for the projects of the Civilian Conservation Corps (CCC). Oregon had sixty-four camps and employed over 12,000 young men. Their masonry and rustic buildings can still be seen all over the state, particularly in forty-five state parks—including Silver Falls State Park, Honeyman State Park, and the Oregon Caves National Monument.

At their peak, the various Tillamook Burns—a series of Oregon forest fires—consumed so much standing timber that charred cinders even rained down at sea. On some beaches, the piles of these cinders were up to two feet deep. In burns between 1933 and 1945, 610,000 acres were leveled by this holocaust.

The Oregon Vortex (or House of Mystery) was established in 1930 in southern Oregon; it may have been the earliest recorded roadside attraction. The Vortex features an anomaly where buildings lean and don't seem to align with gravity. One can still visit it today.

Portland played a pivotal role in the 1934 West Coast waterfront strike, which went on for eighty-two days. In the resulting violence, four were wounded and one killed. The strike was finally won by the International Longshore and Warehouse Union, which ushered in better wages and working conditions for waterfront workers. But the city's business elite fought hard to break it—even hiring 1000 vigilantes to harass the strikers at one point. But the strikers attracted local support too. Their clashes showed that serious issues were at stake.

In 1937, the first transpolar flight from Russia ended in the vicinity of Portland. While hoping to land in San Francisco, the pilots were short of fuel and were having problems with their fuel pump. This caused them to try to land at Portland; however, at the last moment they diverted to Vancouver's Pearson Field across the Columbia when they saw crowds at the Portland airport waiting to hail them as heroes. Recalling that Lindberg's plane was torn apart by fans a decade earlier, when he landed in Paris, they wanted to avoid that fate.

Their trip was a venture watched around the world, as the pilots braved storms, headwinds, ice-covered instruments, and navigational challenges (finding their compass would not work around the North Pole, for instance). Afterwards, they were taken on a cross-country tour, and met the President. Later, they were acclaimed as heroes in the Soviet Union.

CCC Crew at Work

*Things That Give Oregon Character*

In 1937 champion skier Hjalmar Hvam of Portland **invented the first safety ski bindings**. Born in Norway, he had won many early ski championships and coached the US Olympic ski teams. After winning a race at Timberline that year, he broke his leg while skiing. While recuperating, he developed this binding which came into widespread use until the 1960s—the "Saf-Ski" binding. In falls, it broke away easily, minimizing the chances that one's leg would be broken. In fact, it was used in World War II by the Tenth Mountain Division. Hvam was also the first to descend from the top of Mt. Hood on skis.

In late 1941, county officials in southern Oregon and northern California declared that they were withdrawing from their respective states and were setting up the new state of Jefferson. They stopped incoming cars to tell them they were entering this new state, displaying a flag with markings of XX (suggesting this area was being double-crossed by their home states). This was actually just a publicity stunt to generate pressure for better roads, but it has never lost its hold on the local imagination.

Oregon is **one of the few states to still have a Yuba-style gold dredge on location**: the Sumpter Valley Gold Dredge, which stopped operations in 1954 after recovering $4.5 million worth of gold in twenty years of dredging around the clock. It is located a few miles west of Baker City.

The *Spruce Goose* is now at the Evergreen Air Museum in McMinnville, OR. It is **the largest flying boat ever built**, designed and built by Howard Hughes during World War II as the prototype of a heavy transport aircraft (after having first been proposed by Henry J. Kaiser). It was built mostly of birch and pioneering composites, but was not finished in time to be used during that war. But Hughes did get it airborne during a test flight. It has wingspan longer than a football field and is over five stories tall. Financial questions about its status have now been settled.

Portland is one of the few cities that indulges in the mythology of a royal court—choosing princesses and queens—in this case as part of the pageantry of its annual Rose Festival. Established in 1907, its Royal Rosarians act as ambassadors for Portland's Rose Festival and greeters of dignitaries—and march in their white suits and straw hats during the rose parade. These Royal Rosarians select a Prime Minister and Lord High Chancellor—but democratic Rosarians in Portland elect them.

The Rosarians were established by order of the City Council to promote the festival, and are now more than a century old. In 1989, under pressure from the mayor, they were forced to admit women, who now compose a quarter of the group's membership of 275.

Tilikum Crossing Bridge in Portland

Portland is known for over a dozen bridges that cross its rivers and streams; these are unusually varied in terms of construction and style. Among the stationary bridges are:
- the Hawthorne Bridge, Portland's oldest, which uses Parker trusses
- the **Fremont Bridge, the second-largest steel-tied arch bridge in the world**
- the Sellwood Bridge, which uses deck trusses
- the Ross Island Bridge, which uses steel deck trusses
- the Union Pacific Bridge at N.E. 207th Ave., featuring reinforced concrete girders
- the Glenn Jackson Bridge, featuring concrete box girder construction
- the Vista Ave. Viaduct, featuring concrete arches
- the St. John's Bridge: suspension from cables and towers (meaning that the platform on which vehicles move is suspended from cables hung from larger cables strung between the towers)
- **Tilikum Crossing**: a cable-stayed bridge that is the **first limited to light rail, streetcars, busses, bicycles, and pedestrians**; no cars or trucks are permitted

Among the movable bridges are:
- the Hawthorne Bridge—**the oldest vertical lift bridge still operating in the US**

## Oregon: A State That Stands Out

- the Broadway Bridge—a Rall-type, double-leaf, bascule bridge, it had the longest span of this type in the world when it was built in 1913
- the Burnside bridge—a Strauss-type, double-bascule bridge
- the **Steel Bridge** is a railroad bridge, but is the **only telescoping, vertical-lift bridge still operating in the nation**.

Elsewhere in Oregon, a swing-type bridge can still be found in Reedsport on the Umpqua River.

During World War II, a former CCC camp at Waldport became a camp for conscientious objectors. This one was unique because it attracted artists, writers, and musicians and evolved into **the only "fine arts camp" for conscientious objectors**. Dozens of books were produced, as well as a literary journal. While there, poet William Everson wrote a noted book: *The Waldport Poems and War Elegies*. During the war, two other camps for conscientious objectors were set up in Oregon: at Cascade Locks and at Elkton.

MAX Light Rail

Portland has two restored steam-powered locomotives, and one of them (the "Spokane Portland & Seattle 700") is thought to be the **best example in the world of an Art Deco locomotive**. No other city has two operating steam locomotives.

Oregon once experimented with using the chassis of a bus as a kind of gondola to lift skiers to the snowfields on Mt. Hood. In the early 1950s, it ran something called a Skiway Sky Bus—but this was slow and noisy, and as a result, did not last long. While it lasted, however, it was an unusual sight, and the only transport of its kind.

Cannon Beach features one of the longest-running annual sandcastle-building contests. It started in 1954.

Oregon has had rather unique US senators—consider John H. Mitchell, for instance, who was convicted of federal violations in 1905, while still in office. Or Wayne Morse, who served from 1944-1968, and managed to have every possible party affiliation during that time: Republican, Independent, and

Democrat. Morse had also once been the youngest person ever to serve as the Dean of a law school (at the University of Oregon, when he was thirty-one). And for a while he held the filibuster record (speaking on the Senate floor for twenty-two hours and twenty-six minutes).

Many states have a plethora of state symbols, celebrating things that are distinctive about them. But Oregon has an unusually large number of such symbols—over twenty. These include the state father and mother, the state seashell and crustacean, and the state nut. (Oregon is the only state with a state nut: the hazelnut).

Portland is **one of only two US cities to have an aerial tramway** (the other is New York City). It rises 500 feet from the South Waterfront site of Oregon Health & Science University to the university's older buildings on Marquam Hill, offering fine views of Mt. Hood. Built in a cloud of controversy in 2006, it has now carried over ten million riders. It was built by a Swiss firm.

OHSU Tramway in Portland

*Things That Give Oregon Character*

# CHAPTER 5
# GOVERNANCE

LEADER IN REFORMS OF THE PROGRESSIVE ERA

At the time of the Progressive Era (i.e., the early twentieth century), Oregon was a leader in making historic reforms. Often it was the first to adopt such measures, setting the bar for dozens of other states. For a time, **its reforms were known as the "Oregon System"** (indicated below by underlining).

Below is a timeline of key progressive reforms in Oregon, both during the heyday of this movement and after.

**1902:** Oregon adopts William S. U'Ren's proposal for the <u>**initiative and referendum processes**</u>, which enabled citizens to directly initiate laws or amendments to the state's constitution.

U'Ren was a Populist legislator who worked through his Direct Legislation League. Oswald West and C.E.S. Wood both aided him. In due course, this organization became the People's Power League. Members believed that contemporary political processes were controlled by moneyed interests that bribed legislators. Some establishment leaders joined in backing these reforms because they feared a new mass movement of voters indignant over stories of bribery.

In the <u>**initiative process**</u>, the voting public becomes the legislature, creating laws. In the referendum process, the legislature makes the laws it passes conditional on approval by a vote of the people. The public can also trigger a vote on measures that the legislature approves. The effective date of legislation is usually ninety days after passage, except when the legislature claims an emergency, which inhibits use of the referendum.

Of the 340 initiatives proposed by Oregonians since 1902, 118 have been approved. The legislature itself referred 407 measures to a public vote; 233 were approved. Of sixty-two adopted measures subjected to a referendum of the people, twenty-one have been approved.

**1903:** Oregon begins publishing a Voters' Guide to help voters learn about candidates and causes.

That same year, Oregon established its Bureau of Labor to protect workers by enforcing laws like the one that limited the work day for women to 10 hours, and the work week to 60 hours. The Portland Consumers League was instrumental in this law's adoption.

Many labor laws were later challenged in a lawsuit that went to the US Supreme Court, where they were upheld. They were defended by attorney Louis Brandeis, who used social and medical evidence in a (not brief) brief to win his case. This approach was called a "Brandeis Brief." The decision in *Muller v. Oregon (1908)* was the first use of this approach.

**1904:** Oregon adopted the process of having a party's members choose their party's candidates for the primaries (**the Direct Primary Law**). This did not include presidential candidates, however.

**1906:** Oregon adopted the process of **directly choosing its US senators through popular elections** (rather than being done by the legislature). Then the initiative and referendum process was extended to cities.

**1907:** The legislature gave the commissioner of the Bureau of Labor the power to fine employers for failing to remedy hazardous conditions in the workplace and holding them liable for willful violations.

*Governance*

That same year, the Oregon Railroad Commission was re-established to regulate transport and commerce. The first commission had been established in 1885, and then abolished in 1898. Commercial regulation had begun under the Territorial Government in 1849, with regulation of mills and granaries.

**1908:** Oregon's constitution was amended to establish **a process to recall public officials**. That same year saw the creation of the **Corrupt Practices Act**.

**1910:** The Employers' Liability Act was enacted (in civil cases, it required a three-fourths verdict).

**1911:** A Workers Compensation Act, banking laws, and a Public Utility Commission were established.

Oregon decided to begin publishing its informative annual Blue Book. This publication contains a wide variety of information about state government.

**1912:** Oregon's male voters approved **suffrage for women voters**.

Women in Oregon had the right to vote in state elections eight years before the federal government at last gave them the right to vote in its elections. Some fifty suffrage groups organized around the state to press for this vote, including in eastern Oregon. Rural voters were more supportive of women's suffrage, since men in urban areas feared that women voters would push for prohibition. Oregon was **one of eight western states that led the way in giving women the right to vote**.

Prior to this time, supporters of women's rights had already seen some progress in Oregon: in 1866, the state enacted the Married Women's Property Act; in 1887 it gave women the right to vote in school board elections; and in 1885 it allowed women to practice law.

**1912:** an eight-hour workday on public works was established.

**1912:** the state made education compulsory, authorizing the publication of state-produced textbooks.

**1913:** <u>Oregon adopted the process of using the primary for voters to indicate their preferences for their party's nominees in presidential elections</u>.

**1913:** Oregon **was the first state to adopt an enforceable minimum wage law**. Other states copied Oregon's approach; the nation finally did so in 1938. Oregon's law survived legal challenges, and was upheld by both the state and US Supreme Courts.

**1913-14:** <u>Oregon established its workmen's compensation program</u>, which established a fund to compensate those injured in industrial accidents and limited the liability of participating firms. Firms not participating had fewer legal defenses and unlimited liability.

**1914:** Oregon established an 8-hour workday for women and ventilation requirements for work rooms.

**1915:** Oregon voters repealed capital punishment; Governor Oswald West had called for its repeal as early as 1911. However, over the years Oregon has gone back and forth on this issue.

**1919:** Oregon was **the first state to mediate labor/management disputes** through a Board of Conciliation and Arbitration.

**1919:** Oregon was **the first state to establish a gas tax to pay for the state's roads** and highways.

## LEADERSHIP IN LATER REFORMS (POST-PROGRESSIVE ERA)

**1930:** Oregon voters approved setting up Public Utility Districts (bringing in public power to provide competition with private power).

**1949:** A Fair Employment Act for the state was enacted that made it illegal to discriminate in hiring for many reasons, including race or color.

**NOTE**: During the time that the elements of the Oregon System were approved, scholars (who have examined the memorials and resolutions adopted then by the Oregon legislature) have said that they reveal a strong inclination to impose "controls on large businesses."

*Governance*

**1953**: A Public Accommodations Act was passed making it illegal to discriminate in access to public accommodations based on race, color, or religion.

**1959:** A Fair Housing Act was enacted providing penalties for anyone who discriminates in renting or selling real estate.

**1967:** Oregon was the first state to adopt the "prudent man" rule to guide investment of state trust funds so as to optimize returns.

**1972:** When Rep. Edith Green was in Congress (representing Portland), she was instrumental in getting Congress to enact Title IX of the Higher Education Act, opening the way for women in school athletics (she then chaired the Education and Labor committee).

**1981:** Oregon pioneered experimenting with choosing members of the legislature by mailed ballot. In 1998, it was extended to all matters subject to a vote. Oregon is now the **only state where voting is entirely by mail**. In recent elections, 85 percent of registered voters have voted in the general election—**the highest rate in the nation**. In 2015, Oregon decided to register qualified, but unregistered voters, when they renew their drivers' licenses (unless they indicate they don't want to be registered).

**1984:** Oregon established its Citizens' Utility Board, which is a watchdog board to protect the interests of consumers in setting rates for electricity, gas, and telephone charges.

**1985:** Oregon was the first state to set up a fund to compensate workers of firms that go out of business while owing wages.

**1994:** With the Oregon Health Plan adopted this year, Oregon became the **first state to provide health care to its uninsured citizens**.

**1998:** Oregon was the **first state to adopt a program that permits physician-assisted suicide for those in terminal condition**; it was originated by Dr. Peter

Goodwin and was called Death with Dignity. 341 patients have chosen to use it, including Dr. Goodwin who had a fatal brain disease.

**2002:** Oregon voters approved an initiative to automatically increase the state's minimum wage with inflationary increases in the CPI. Now it is **among the highest in the nation**.

**2011:** The Oregon legislature established a review of proposed initiatives in every election by a demographically balanced panel that is randomly selected. That panel assesses the possible impacts of an initiative and makes recommendations to voters (Citizens Initiative Review); it is designed to counterbalance the impact of special-interest money.

**2014:** Oregon led the nation in making key birth certificates and other documents available to adults who have been adopted, without their having to go to court.

**2015:** Oregon closed loopholes on required background checks for the sale of guns so that now such checks here cover all transactions (i.e., **universal background checks**). Oregon is one of only six states requiring such checks.

## OTHER INFORMATION ABOUT GOVERNANCE

**Oregon is one of five states with no sales tax**, which its voters have repeatedly turned down. It is viewed as a regressive tax.

The state's constitutional provisions guaranteeing free expression (Art. 1, sec. 8) are broader than those at the federal level, and have even been interpreted to override laws banning obscenity (Oregon is the first and only state to have done that). A recent survey named Portland as the "kinkiest" city in the country. Perhaps there is a connection.

When Dave Frohnmayer was state Attorney General in the 1980s, many thought the state's Department of Justice was the best in the country (see comments of associate William Gary).

*Governance*

Oregon: A State That Stands Out

When Richard Neuberger was a US Senator from Oregon (1955-1960), he was a leader in pressing successfully for a federal program to restrict billboards along interstate freeways. The federal government provided bonuses to states that adopted standard control regulations. When Neuberger was succeeded by his wife, Maurine (1960-1966), she worked to extend that program. She also provided the national leadership to put health warnings on packages of cigarettes.

Oregon is a **top-rated state in terms of the transparency of its budgetary transactions** (it was second in 2014).

In a Likert Scale evaluation of its voting patterns, Oregon has been characterized as the most politically polarized state—having both the most liberal and conservative voters (a finding in the 2004 election).

Robert Putnam of Harvard asserts that Portland (and possibly Oregon) **has one of the highest rates of civic engagement**.

Baker City may be in the best fiscal condition in the state. Benefactor Leo Adler, a Baker City native who went on to make a fortune distributing magazines, left his fortune to a community fund that supports civic and municipal improvement projects there. At his death, his legacy was worth over $20 million.

## CHAPTER 6

# GEOGRAPHIC FEATURES

Oregon's **geographic center is farther west than that of any of the other contiguous states**. The westernmost incorporated community in the contiguous United States is Port Orford. The westernmost lighthouse is in Oregon on Cape Blanco, and the westernmost railroad lines (connected to a national network) are those running to Coos Bay (long. 124.21667 W).

Water, wind, and volcanic activity have shaped Oregon's landscape and given it many distinctive features.

### WATER

For instance, these forces have given us the **country's deepest canyon**—Hells Canyon, which is 7993 feet deep; and the **country's deepest lake**—Crater Lake, which is nearly 2000 feet deep. Of lakes above sea level, Crater Lake is the deepest in the world.

Oregon has a geological feature that is rare for the US: major rivers—the **Willamette** and the **Deschutes—that flow straight northward**. According to *Guinness World Records*, it is also home to one of the two shortest rivers—the D River in Lincoln City. (The other is in Montana.)

Some parts of **Oregon's Coast Range get as much rainfall as anywhere** in the contiguous states—180-200 inches annually.

Oregon also has notable lakes:

Michael McCloskey | 55

**Klamath Lake is one of the largest freshwater lakes in the West**.

**Waldo Lake is one of the clearest and purest lakes in the US**.

The **Columbia River** has **the largest volume of water flowing into the Pacific Ocean** of any river in North America. The area around its mouth has **some of the roughest sea conditions in the world**. It has been called the "Graveyard of the Pacific": 2000 large ships have been lost there since 1792.

Oregon has **the most waterfalls of any state**—226—and the **Columbia Gorge** has the highest concentration of them on the continent (seventy-seven on the Oregon side alone).

The Columbia Gorge is widely regarded as **one of the most outstanding gorges in the world** in terms of scenery, geology, and biodiversity (800 species of plants can be found there, 15 of which are rare or endangered). It also has one of the nation's highest waterfalls: Multnomah Falls, at 620 feet. The Travel Channel named the gorge as one of the "Top Ten Wonders of the West."

And just taking into account waterfalls entirely in the US, **Willamette Falls has the greatest volume of water flowing over it**. Celilo Falls on the Columbia once had the largest flow rate on the continent, and the sixth largest in the world. It has since been flooded by the Dalles Dam.

The **largest meteorite ever found in the US** was found in Oregon in the early twentieth century. Weighing 15.5 tons, it is now displayed in the Museum of Natural History in New York City. It is thought to have been swept into the Willamette Valley by the Missoula Floods 12-18,000 years ago. Flowing down the Columbia into the Willamette Valley, some think these floods may have carried the greatest discharge of waters of all time.

## VOLCANIC ACTIVITY

Eastern Oregon is the center of a huge sheet of basaltic lava—the largest in the US. Known as **the Columbia Plateau Lava Flow**, most it of it flowed out 14-17 million years ago. These are **the world's deepest lava flows**—greater than 2000 feet in places.

The heaviest concentration of vents and volcanoes in the country is in the Oregon Cascades. It is the heart of the West Coast's volcanic features.

At under two thousand years of age, the lava fields on the McKenzie Pass are the newest major flow in the contiguous US, covering seventy square miles.

**Newberry Crater and environs have the most varied formations of lava flows in the US.** Newberry has one of the world's largest calderas—4 x 5 miles in diameter (second only to Crater Lake). Its Big Obsidian flow is the world's most extensive obsidian formation. (Diamond Crater, further east in Oregon—just south of Malheur Lake—has the most varied forms of basalt.)

Mt. Mazama (the extinct volcano that produced Crater Lake) once ejected more pumice than any other volcano in the world.

## OTHER GEOLOGIC FORCES / MISCELLANY

Klamath Falls is underlain by the largest geothermal reservoir of hot water and steam in the Western Hemisphere.

Oregon is one of the few states with geysers. A few miles north of Lakeview, in eastern Oregon, Old Perpetual Geyser periodically shoots hot water sixty feet into the air.

Oregon has 125 hot springs, some of which—Belknap Springs, Breitenbush Hot Springs, Bagby Hot Springs, and Hart Mountain Hot Springs, for instance—are used for recreation. At one time, the most celebrated hot springs were those at the Hot Lake Hotel, northwest of the town of Union, in eastern Oregon. Over time, it evolved into a major resort attracting a worldwide clientele. By the 1920s, it had room for over 1000 guests who could arrive by rail. Among notable guests were the Mayo brothers. Part of the complex was destroyed by fire in 1934—but some of its buildings remain, and activities there continue.

Of the caves protected under the aegis of the National Park Service, **the caves in Oregon Caves National Monument are among the finest made of marble.** They were once called the "Marble Halls of Oregon."

*Geographic Features*

Oregon is one of the best places to look for the sort of geological oddities that are sometimes produced by volcanic activity. These include obsidian (black glass), thunder eggs (agate in cavities of welded tuff), agates (quartz), and sunstones (gem-quality feldspars with minute copper platelets). Productive places to look for them include: Glass Butte in central Oregon (for obsidian); Madras (for thunder eggs); and Agate Beach, north of Newport (for agates). Sunstones can be found in small outcrops of basalt (such as those just east of Abert Rim).

**The John Day Fossil Beds National Monument displays the longest period of geological time of any US fossil bed** (forty million years). It is acknowledged to exhibit the richest concentration of prehistoric fossils.

**Abert Rim is the highest fault escarpment in North America**: it rises 2000 feet from the desert floor. Steens Mountain is the largest fault block in the northern Great Basin.

The largest monolith in Oregon is Wolf Rock, in the upper drainage of Blue River in the Willamette National Forest. It rises majestically 1000 feet above the surrounding forest. Since it is even larger than Haystack Rock on the coast (which is internationally ranked), it is probably internationally noteworthy. Another noteworthy monolith in the state is Stein's Pillar, which rises 300 feet above the forests east of Prineville.

Oregon is one of the few states with mima mounds—a mysterious form of patterned ground. They can be seen beside Lower Table Rock, near Medford.

Oregon is home to one of the coldest places in the United States: the town of Seneca, located in Grant County at the northern edge of the Great Basin. In February of 1933, it got as cold as fifty-four degrees below Fahrenheit there. This makes it one of the ten coldest places in the lower forty-eight states.

## COASTLINE

The nearly unrelenting winds along the Oregon coast have built **the nation's longest coastal-dune complex**—running for fifty miles south of Florence.

Oregon's Sea Lion Caves are **the world's largest sea caves**, located on a beach that has been around since the ice age. They are the only mainland-breeding site of Stellar sea lions: several hundred breed there.

**Haystack Rock**, near Cape Kiwanda, **is one of the largest coastal monoliths in the world**—in fact, it is the fourth largest, at 327 feet.

At Thor's Well, near Cape Perpetua, one can see an amazing sight. During winter storms, as the tidal currents batter the rocks, the ocean appears to be flowing into a well. This is a phenomenon powered by the Pacific's tidal surges during high tides. One writer called it one of the six oddest natural wonders.

## BIOLOGY

Oregon has thirteen national forests—more than any other Pacific Northwest state—covering over sixteen million acres. When many of those along the Cascades were set aside in 1893 as the Cascade Forest Reserve, it was the largest such reserve of its time—at 4.8 million acres. The Rogue River-Siskiyou National Forest is regarded as having biodiversity of world-class importance; 400 of its plants are classified as having such importance.

Oregon has one of the few National Grasslands not on the Great Plains, and certainly the westernmost of them: the Crooked River National Grasslands (at 112,357 acres).

Oregon also has one of the largest long-term ecological research sites in the country: the H. J. Andrews Experimental Forest (USFS) in the Willamette National Forest.

The wild horses that thrive in the Kiger Gorge, in the Steens Mountain area, are thought to display a heritage as Spanish mustangs. They have similar color characteristics (the "dun factor") and show genetic connections. **These horses comprise the third largest band of free-roaming wild horses in the country.**

The mild climate of western Oregon, particularly Portland, makes it one of the best locations for growing trees and plants from around the world.

*Geographic Features*

**Oregon supports a more diverse range of forest species than elsewhere in the US**—with thirty different species of conifers (including eight species of pines). Oregon has six of the seven species of true firs that grow in North America—more than any other state.

**Portland's Hoyt Arboretum**, established in 1928, **displays the largest assembly of conifers of any arboretum in the US.**

A puzzling 9000-acre stand of ponderosa pines is found on Bureau of Land Management (BLM) territory, ten miles northeast of Christmas Valley, in eastern Oregon. Growing far away from any other stand, on pumice gravel, in a place where it gets only half the rainfall such trees require, it nonetheless thrives. It is known as the Lost Forest.

**Oregon** (where three floristic provinces overlap) **is the heart of conifer country.** It is a state where species from the south (e.g., the Jeffrey pine) coexist with species from the north (e.g., noble fir). It also has species from the Rocky Mountain region further east (e.g., paper birch, in the Wallowa Mountains).

To elaborate further:

In the southern Cascades and the Siskiyous are found species from the California Floristic Province: California red fir, sugar pine, tanoaks, California laurels, and coastal redwoods. Some think the Siskiyou Mountains have the most diverse collection of conifers in the world.

The southern Cascades also host a hybrid of California's red fir and the noble fir: the Shasta fir, which grows above 4500 feet.

Noble fir, Sitka spruce, Alaska cedar, and various true firs come from the north.

Eastern Oregon's Junipers are more characteristic of the Great Basin, and the Wallowas have trees from the Rocky Mountains, such as the Rocky Mountain form of Douglas fir.

Oregon is **the only West Coast state where tree species from the south and north overlap** so that hybridization can occur.

Several Oregon trees have been listed as "national champions" by the American Forestry Association (AFA). The association's ranking scores are formulated by adding together the height, diameter, and crown breadth of each tree being evaluated. Oregon is among the top ten in its rankings.

At this time, the tallest living Douglas fir is the Doerner Fir, which stands at 329 feet in Coos County (on BLM land). A Douglas fir nearly as tall has been located in the Lowell District of the Willamette National Forest (it is 322 feet tall). The giant ponderosa pine in the La Pine State Recreation Area has at various times been the AFA champion; it has a circumference of 348 inches.

The tallest ponderosa pine is in the Rogue River-Siskiyou National Forest; it stands at 268 feet.

The one-time champion Sitka spruce tree at Klootchy Creek, near Seaside, fell in a storm in 2007. It had a diameter of 16.7 feet. Other huge Oregon trees remain: one at Cape Meares (with a diameter of 15.27 feet) and one at Falcon's Tower near Manzanita (with a diameter of 13.51 feet).

A limber pine—on Cusick Mountain in the Wallowas—is thought to be the third-oldest in the world; it is probably over 2000 years old. Its diameter is 81 inches.

Among other AFA champions in Oregon are a Port Orford cedar in the Siskiyou National Forest (219 feet tall); a Brewer spruce in Josephine County; a Baker cypress in the Rogue River National Forest; a knobcone pine in Josephine County; a tanoak in Curry County; a cascara buckthorn in Curry County; a Giant chinkapin in Douglas County; an Oregon white oak in Douglas County; a black cottonwood in Mission State Park, Marion County; a white alder and a Western dogwood in Polk County; a Hooker willow in Tillamook County; a bigleaf maple, a Pacific dogwood, and an Oregon ash in Multnomah County; a water birch in Wallowa County; and a silver buffaloberry in Malheur County.

Some of Oregon's champion tree specimens are not native to the region. For instance, the country's largest black walnut is in Multnomah County; its largest plum tree is in Klamath county; and its largest American chestnut is in the town of Sherwood, on Edy Road. In 1860, the pioneers planted a cherry tree in Eugene that has since attained an immense size. Many think this Black Tartar-

Champion Sitka Spruce at Klootchy Creek near Seaside

*Geographic Features*

ian cherry is the biggest in the country—certainly in Oregon. (Its cherries are very good!)

Oregon also has record-sized specimens of Pacific rhododendrons (in Lane County), big sagebrush (in Jefferson County), Pacific red elderberry (in Tillamook County), and buffaloberry (in Malheur County).

**The largest single organism in the world** is in the Malheur National Forest: the fungus, *Armillaria solidipes*.

Some plants and animals are found only in Oregon—so-called endemics. For instance, one kind of rough-skinned newt (known as the Mazama Newt) has been found in Crater Lake National Park. At the top of Mary's Peak, one can find the Mary's Peak salamander. In the Siskiyou-Klamath region, 280 endemics are found—many of them in Oregon.

Among Oregon's endemic plants are the:
- Port Orford cedar: SW Oregon
- Kalmiopsis: in Kalmiopsis Wilderness in SW Oregon
- Green-flowered Wild Ginger: found only in the Siskiyou area
- Steens Mountain thistle: found in the Pueblo Mountains in SE OR
- Steens draba
- Steens Mountain paintbrush
- Wallowa paintbrush
- Pale Wallowa paintbrush
- Sticky paintbrush
- Peacock larkspur
- Dwarf meadowfoam
- Wooly meadowfoam
- Parry's townsendia
- White Mule's Ears
- Greene's mariposa lily
- Bruneau mariposa lily
- Howell's mariposa

- Pumice sandwort
- Ashland lupine
- Owyhee clover
- Packard's blazingstar
- Short-leaved cinquefoil
- Cusick's camas
- Oregon fetid adder's tongue
- Gentner's fritillary

Many endemics are found in the Rough and Ready area south of Cave Junction; the Siskiyou region has one-quarter of Oregon's rare and endangered species. Some of the endemics are on the state list of endangered and threatened species (e.g., Peacock larkspur).

Oregon's endemic butterflies are the:

- Oregon silverspot
- Leona's little blue butterfly
- Fender's blue
- Mission blue

The state is also home to an endemic dragonfly: the Bison snaketail.

Oregon is **among the nation's top five states in terms of bird diversity**; some 500 avian species spend some time in the state.

The Zumwalt Prairie, east of the Wallowas, provides habitat for one of the nation's largest populations of nesting raptors.

Chapman Elementary School in Portland is the nation's top roosting spot for swifts.

In the contiguous US, Oregon provides one of the few places where one can easily see rare birds (such as Tufted puffins on Haystack Rock near Cannon Beach, and trumpeter swans on the lower Columbia River, or on ponds near the site of the former Trojan nuclear plant). Wood ducks—gorgeous and

Oregon: A State That Stands Out

elusive—can easily be seen on the ponds at the Crystal Springs Rhododendron Garden in Portland.

The Nestucca Bay unit of the Oregon Coast National Wildlife Refuge provides the wintering ground for the entire world population of the Semidi Islands Aleution Cackling Goose.

The writer, conservationist, and angler Jack Hemingway called **the North Umpqua River "the greatest stretch of summer steelhead water in the United States."**

And **the lower Columbia River has the largest, healthiest population of white sturgeons on the continent** (the sturgeon is the largest freshwater ascending fish in North America). They can reach fifteen feet in length and can weigh more than a thousand pounds.

Certain indigenous chubs are found only at particular places in Oregon: the Alvord chub, below Steens Mountain; the Warner sucker, below Hart Mountain; the Klamath Lake sculpin, above Klamath Falls; the Lost River and shortnose suckers, in the upper Klamath Basin; the Borax Lake chub, at Borax Lake; and the Oregon chub, in the Willamette Valley.

Depoe Bay in Lincoln County is known as "**the whale watching capital of the world**," since crowds gather there to see some of the 20,000 Gray whales that pass by closely as they migrate north and south along the coast; it even has a pod of whales that resides in the area. Locals also claim that Depoe Bay is the world's smallest, navigable harbor.

## CELEBRATED GARDENS

The International Rose Test Garden, in Portland's Washington Park, features over 600 varieties of roses, and 10,000 rose bushes. It is the **oldest continuously operated public rose test garden in the country**, and has won an International Award for Excellence. It was established in 1917, in cooperation with the American Rose Society. The Portland Rose Society hosts the

**longest-running rose show in the country**; now in its second century, the show is part of the Rose Festival.

Portland's first public rose garden was in Peninsula Park, established in 1909 and the site of the annual rose show until 1917. It is a formal, two-acre park with over 5700 rose plants and seventy-five varieties. Most of the roses are in a sunken garden, with brick walkways and an ornamental fountain at its center. Some think it is Oregon's most beautiful garden. Its nearby octagonal bandstand is on the National Register.

Peninsula Park in Portland

Portland also has an impressive nine-acre rhododendron garden: the Crystal Springs Rhododendron Garden, featuring over 2500 rhododendrons and azaleas from ninety-four species—many over fifty years old. It is interspersed with many natural water features.

Perched on a bluff on the west bank of the Willamette River, the Elk Rock Gardens of the Bishop's Close have an interesting history. Peter Kerr, a businessman who emigrated from Scotland, developed the site under the guidance of noted landscape architect John Olmsted. The nine acres of gardens feature many rare species of magnolias, as well as spectacular views of Mt. Hood. The gardens were created in 1897 and may be the largest private gardens in the PNW that are still intact.

**Portland's Japanese Garden** is draped over 5.5 acres on the West Hills. It is appreciated for its authenticity. Japan's ambassador thought it "**the most authentic Japanese garden**, including those in Japan" (2011). It has also been praised by the *Journal of Japanese Gardening*, which in 2004 ranked it highly.

Oregon: A State That Stands Out

Portland Japanese Garden

**Portland's Lan Su Chinese Garden** was set up in 1999 by 65 artisans from Suzhou, in China. It is regarded as the **most authentic Chinese garden** outside of China. It is a walled garden, with a pond, a teahouse, covered walkways, and bridges. It has over 400 plant species, specializing in those that are common to China. As of this writing, most of its plants are still gaining in size and establishing needed balance with the garden's stone structures. Over time, it will become even more inviting.

A spectacular "garden for all seasons" is found at Shore Acres State Park on the coast near Coos Bay. Shipbuilder Louis J. Simpson planted seven acres of formal gardens around his mansion there. The mansion burned in 1921, but the gardens survived and have been groomed as a state park. Because of the area's mild climate, flowers are in bloom there all year long.

The Oregon Garden near Silverton was developed at the behest of Oregon Association of Nurseries. While it has an ample land base (80 acres) and has been laid out professionally, most of its plants are still too young to be of great interest, as the garden only opened in 1999. But it does use reclaimed wastewater to irrigate its grounds.

Oddly enough, one of the finest ornamental flowers visible among state parks along the northern Oregon coast is the foxglove, which features clusters of purple and white flowers on long stems. However, it happens to be an exotic plant, and is not native to Oregon. It was brought here by English families working for the Hudson Bay Company at Fort Vancouver. However, it is now seen as having become "naturalized."

## CHAPTER 7

# ENVIRONMENTAL CONSERVATION

### ENVIRONMENT

Looked at on a per capita basis, Oregon is **the greenest state in terms of programs to protect the environment**.

It is **the only state with a comprehensive land-use planning system**. This has been of material help in preventing the loss of fertile farm soils.

It was **the first state to clean up a major river**, making it meet all federal water pollution standards (viz., the Willamette River in 1972).

Oregon was also **the first state to set up an Air Pollution Authority** (in 1951) in the hope of making the air cleaner. This was done after the public began to criticize air pollution coming from aluminum-reduction plants.

Since 2011, the state has **implemented the strongest restrictions on the levels of toxic chemicals permitted in its waters**. In 2015, it also required a phase-out of toxic materials in products used particularly by children.

In 1975, Oregon became **the first jurisdiction in the world to ban CFCs in aerosols** to protect the ozone layer.

It was also the **first state to adopt a mandatory bottle-deposit law**, which has been steadily expanded. In the early 1970s, Oregon led the process of banning detachable pull-tabs on metal beverage containers; these bans spread throughout the world, as these tabs posed a vexing litter problem.

Michael McCloskey

Oregon: A State That Stands Out

Under Governor Tom McCall, Oregon achieved so many milestones in environmental progress that, by the mid-1970s, **McCall was traveling the country, telling what he called "the Oregon Story."** Most importantly, he had kindled pride in the task of protecting the state's environment. Some felt his efforts had put Oregon on the national map for the first time since its "Oregon System" of initiatives and referenda, established seventy years before (see such suggestions in *Oregon's Promise* by historian David Peterson de Mar).

Oregon is **one of the top states in its rates of recycling waste material**.

Oregon has **been ranked nationally as among the best states in terms of the cleanliness of its roadsides** and lack of litter.

Oregon is **ranked fourth in terms of its progress in gaining greater energy efficiency**. On a per capita basis, Oregonians have the fifth lowest level of greenhouse gas emissions. In 1993, Portland became the first American city to develop a local climate action plan.

Oregon is **among the top five states in terms of installed wind capacity**—a total of 3153 megawatts.

Oregon is **one of the few states to practically rule out nuclear power from its future power supply**. The state passed an initiative in 1980, making it unlikely that another nuclear plant will ever be built here. In the early nineties, it closed down the only one that it had: the Trojan Nuclear Power Plant.

Portland's utility—Pacific Gas and Electric Company (PGE)—has **the most successful program to encourage greater use of renewable power**: in terms of the number of its customers, total sales, and the percentage of its customers choosing that option. By 2040, its utilities must derive at least half their power from renewable sources.

Oregon has **one of the best networks of public charging stations for electric cars**, with 900 of them currently on the road, and more being added all the time.

On a per capita basis, Portland has the most publicly available charging stations for electric vehicles.

Electric Car Charging Station

68 | CHAPTER 7

Oregon ranks second in terms of states making use of federal grants to build light rail systems.

Portland has some of the purest drinking water in the country.

In 2012, Oregon Senator Jeff Merkley was the only Senator to earn a League of Conservation Voters rating of 100 percent for his support of environmental positions.

Oregon is **now the leading promoter of sustainability**, with many green industries and Leadership in Energy & Environmental Design (LEED) certified buildings. By 2013, Oregon was among the top ten states in LEED-certified construction projects (based on environmental standards). For instance, in 2002 grape producer Sokol Blosser built the first LEED-certified winery in the country. A list of the 100 greenest businesses in Oregon is published each year—this list includes software and high tech firms, hotels, and major law firms.

In a recent survey **of the fifty greenest US cities, Portland was ranked number one**[5], and Eugene number five.

Oregon **was the first state to issue pollution emission limits for wood stoves**. The EPA has now set an even stronger standard.

**Portland has been listed as the best city for public transportation.**

It **was the first city to tear up and remove a freeway** (Harbor Drive, removed in 1970 by order of Governor Tom McCall). Its new Orange Light Rail Line is the first in the world to plant green ground cover (i.e., grass and other low-lying vegetative material) between the tracks.

One survey judged Portland, Oregon to be the **second-most bicycle-friendly city in the world** (the first was Minneapolis, Minnesota). It is also a hub of American bicycle manufacturing: over forty firms build bicycles in Portland.

Oregon is **the first state to set up a network of "state scenic bikeways"** (at the behest of Cycle Oregon). In 1971, the state of Oregon decided to set aside one percent of its highway funds for constructing bicycle paths; fourteen of them have been designated. The annual Cycle Oregon-sponsored ride around different parts of the state has been described as the "best bike ride in America."

---

[5] See 2012 survey by Professor Kent Portney (of Tufts University) for the Canadian magazine *Corporate Knights*.

*Environmental Conservation*

Eugene, Oregon now leads the nation in the percentage of its citizens who commute by bicycle (8.3 percent). Portland is in fourth place, with 6 percent.

Portland has been listed **among the top ten cities in the US for walking**. Its residents drive about twenty percent less than most Americans.

Two of Oregon's three law schools are known for their specialties in environmental law: the University of Oregon and Lewis & Clark.

In 2015, the Princeton Review rated Lewis & Clark the most sustainable university in the nation (in terms of practices, policies, and academic offerings).

## CONSERVATION

Public rights to use Oregon beaches were established at an early date (1913); all offshore rocks and islands also are now federal waterfowl refuges.

Oregon is the only state with such a determined policy to provide access to its public beaches. On the average, every three miles the State Parks Department provides a corridor through private property to reach state-owned beaches.

Oregon has forty-seven wilderness areas; only four states have more. Eighteen percent of the national forest land in Oregon has been designated as wilderness.

Twenty-seven percent of Oregon's forests have been reserved in one way or another (either administratively or by statute) and that figure is unlikely ever to be cut. A little over half of the remaining forestland supporting large trees (i.e., over twenty inches in diameter near the base of the trunk) has been reserved.

Oregon has **the most federally designated wild rivers**: forty-nine river reaches, encompassing 1800 miles of stream length.

Oregon has **the world's only full-service police laboratory specializing in wildlife forensics**, protecting species that are endangered or threatened. Since 1989, the US Fish and Wildlife Service has operated it in Ashland. With a large bank of wildlife tissue samples, it uses infrared spectroscopy and electron microscopes to do its analyses. It helps prosecute those suspected of smuggling, poaching, hunting, or importing protected wildlife. It also manages the National Eagle Repository.

Four conservation organizations that work at the national or regional level are based in Oregon: the Xerces Society (working to protect butterflies and other invertebrates), Forest Service Employees for Environmental Ethics, Ecotrust, and the Pacific Rivers Council.

In 2015, the Humane Society of the United States rated Oregon as **one of the most animal-friendly states**.

**The state's shrimp industry was the first anywhere to be certified as sustainable** (by the Marine Stewardship Council).

Oregon has **pioneered a number of innovative formulas to protect special areas**. For instance, it was the first state to have a National Monument established for its biodiversity alone: the Cascade-Siskiyou National Monument. This features an incredibly diverse habitat for butterflies.

The formula used to protect the Steens Mountain complex (officially known as the Steens Mountain Cooperative Management and Protection Area) includes a combination of wilderness, wild and scenic rivers, wildlife reserves, and areas closed to grazing and mining (this was the first time grazing was banned on BLM lands).

The varied zones within the Columbia Gorge Scenic Area—which have been set aside for nature protection, farming and forestry, and urban development—are another example of such innovation. All development and logging within the Scenic Area must be consistent with protecting its natural values. The Scenic Area spans two states.

Additionally, there is the Redband Trout Reserve, set up in connection with the designation of the Steens complex).

Oregon is **among the top ten states in the amount of public use of its state park system**—and this has been true for quite some time. Its parks are among the most intensively used. The long-time director of the state park system, David Talbot, held the record as the longest-serving such official in the

## Oregon: A State That Stands Out

Lithia Park in Ashland

country. Talbot's service was recognized when he was given the Pugsley Medal—a national award for distinguished service.

Oregon has **the largest forested municipal park**: Portland's Forest Park (5157 acres).

Portland's Heritage Tree program protects large, old trees. Over 300 have been saved so far.

Portlanders attain top ranking in terms of the amount they spend on natural foods, gardening, and the outdoors.

In 2014, Ashland's Lithia Park was **named as one of the Ten Great Public Spaces in America** by the American Planning Association. Its varied assembly of trees and shrubs puts it in a category by itself.

Bend's Drake Park, with a half mile of frontage on Mirror Pond (which is an impoundment of an upper portion of the Deschutes River), is certainly one of the state's most popular city parks. Other well-loved city parks along major rivers are: Riverside Park in Grants Pass (along the Rogue River), Skinner's Butte Park in Eugene (along the Willamette River), Riverfront Park in Salem (also along the Willamette River), and Tom McCall Waterfront Park in Portland (also along the Willamette River).

Some assert that Curry County's coastline is one of the most scenic in the world (the National Park Service once tried to turn a stretch of it into a national park). One story by *National Geographic* magazine listed the Columbia Gorge as one of the most popular tourist destinations. And in 2013 Cannon Beach was listed by *National Geographic* as one of the 100 most beautiful places in the world.

One of the country's most spectacular urban views is available to those traveling along State Street in Hood River. One can look out on a spectacular close-up view of Mt. Adams, as well as having a splendid view of the Columbia River below.

The area around Portland is the only urban setting in the contiguous states having views of five major glacier-clad mountains. They are: Mt. Hood, Mt. St. Helens, Mt. Adams, Mt. Jefferson, and Mt. Rainier.

**CHAPTER 8**

# NATURAL RESOURCES AND AGRICULTURE

### FOREST PRODUCTS

Oregon is **still the leading producer of softwood lumber** (4.2 billion board feet in 2013). Back in 1953, it produced nearly ten billion board feet, with over 1500 mills. At that time, the timber industry supported as many as 80,000 jobs in the state; now it only supports about 7500. Even in the early twentieth century, logging towns were coming and going: seventy-six had disappeared from the northwest by then.

One firm that is still thriving is Roseburg Forest Products—the largest family-owned wood products company in the country. The Seneca Sawmill in Eugene is also one of the largest in the country, producing 650 million board feet of Douglas fir lumber each year. In the mid-1920s, the largest Ponderosa pine mills in the world were in Bend: Brooks-Scanlon and Shevlin-Hixon. At times of peak production, Oregon had as many as seventy plywood mills.

In the heyday of Oregon timbering, logging trucks used to creep through the streets of towns on their way to mills. Often they carried only one huge log—sometimes five feet in diameter. One Douglas fir measured sixteen feet in diameter; a round from what is known as "the Clatsop fir" can be seen in Collier Memorial State Park on Highway 97 north of Klamath Falls. At the time it was produced, loggers were cutting the best of the old growth.

Oregon: A State That Stands Out

Log Raft on River (Historic)

Rafts of logs used to be seen on Oregon's rivers. At the time, Oregon law required that the logs be branded to indicate who owned them; all these brands were registered with the state. This was a process similar to branding cattle. These rafts used to be towed out into the ocean and hauled to places such as San Francisco.

Oregon is **the leading producer of Christmas trees**; 6.1 million are grown here each year.

## FARMS AND FISHERIES

Oregon grows 240 specialty crops, with a harvest that is among the most diverse of any state. Diversity has various advantages, such as minimizing insect infestations. Cranberries are one of the state's specialty crops, grown on the southern Oregon coast (south of Coos Bay). Because of the moderate climate of the area and its long growing season, these berries are sweeter and darker than those grown in other states. Oregon is **among the top cranberry-producing states** (currently, it is fourth). It is also the leading state in the production of peppermint for peppermint oil. A great variety of herbs are grown in the state; over 300 can be obtained from the Blue Heron Herbary on Sauvie Island. The Siskiyou Rare Plant Nursery in Medford also has rare alpine plants, among others.

Oregon is **near the top spot in terms of farm sales directly to consumers** ($15 per consumer, per shopping trip—second only to Vermont); sixteen percent of all farmers in Oregon sell directly to consumers, as opposed to about six percent nationally. These sales occur at the 120 farmers markets now spread across Oregon, which are a key part of the local-food movement.

Oregon is **one of the top states too in terms of sale of organic farm products** and its acreage in organic crops.

Oregon is **the center of the shrimp industry on the West Coast**, now producing seventy-five percent of the landings there ("landings" here refers to the number of shrimp caught and brought to shore). Of the various West Coast ports, six of those in Oregon are top-rated in terms of the size and value of their seafood landings. The seafood industry in Oregon is faring better than in neighboring states. Newport is regarded as having the "best working waterfront on the West Coast." Since the largest tonnage of Dungeness crabs is landed there, it also calls itself the "Dungeness crab capital of the world."

## WINES, OLIVE OIL, AND CHEESES

Oregon is **now a world-class producer of Pinot Noir wines**. "Oregon's Pinot Noir wines are second to none in this country," *Wine Spectator* magazine proclaimed in 2012. As early as 1980, the state was winning competitions in France. The winery at the King Estate, south of Eugene, is the biggest producer of Pinot Noir wines in the state. Over half the wines made in Oregon are Pinot Noir wines.

Oregon now has 905 vineyards planted on over 19,000 acres of land. It has 800 licensed wineries **and ranks third in terms of the amount of wine produced**. In 2015, Oregon's wine production was thought to have an economic value of over $3 billion (direct and indirect); case sales here earn the highest average return in the country. Sales at the tasting rooms of its wineries are soaring, as are tours of its wine country—which are thought to contribute over $200 million to the state's economy. One of the ten best wine areas in which to travel, according to *Wine Enthusiast* magazine, is southern Oregon, such as in Douglas County, which recently won twenty-eight medals for its wine in a national competition.

**Oregon has the strictest wine-labeling laws in the US**: Oregon wines must contain not less than ninety percent of the varietal wine on the label.

Stoller Vineyard near Dundee

The northernmost commercial olive groves are found in Oregon—near Dayton, where 13,000 olive trees are flourishing. The Oregon Olive Mill there produces olive oil (including Koroneika Extra Virgin Olive Oil).

In recent years, Oregon's artisanal cheesemakers have won international recognition and awards (as in 2007, 2009, and 2011). In 2014, Rivers Edge Chèvre (produced at the Three Ring Farm in Logsden, Oregon) was **rated as the best American cheese** at the International Cheese Awards in Nantwich, England. Face Rock Creamery in Bandon has also won first-place awards for its cheddars. And even Oregon's largest cheese maker, Tillamook Cheese, won an international award in 2010 for its cheddar (at the World Cheese Championship Contest). A group to promote cheeses made in the state has now been organized: the Oregon Cheese Guild.

## SPECIALTY CROPS

The Northwest produces one-quarter of the world's hops. Oregon was the leading state in **hop production** until 1943 (it is **now ranked second**), when a blight caused production to drop. However, that is no longer a problem. As demand grows, plantings are again increasing.

Oregon **produces the most truffles in the US**, backed by almost a century of agricultural research at Oregon State University. It is one of the few places in the world that not only grows black truffles, but has its own native species of truffles—white truffles. And now it even has a truffle festival (and is the only state with an event like this).

Millions of dollars of worth of Matsutake mushrooms come from Oregon, mainly for export to Japan. They are found in stands of pine in various national forests, including the Deschutes, Umpqua, Winema-Fremont, and Willamette forests. Morel mushrooms are also sought in these forests, for the domestic market.

Oregon is **virtually the nation's only producer of hazelnuts**, and the world's third-largest producer of them. This crop was brought to Oregon in the late 1840s by Henderson Luelling. Major plantings began near Springfield in 1903.

The Hermiston area of eastern Oregon produces some of the country's sweetest watermelons.

The process of brining cherries to produce maraschino cherries was developed in 1927 by Professor Ernest Weigand at Oregon State University. Also in 1956, OSU researcher George Waldo developed the marionberry as a hybrid of hybrids. It is now the most widely grown kind of blackberry in Oregon.

Garlic is grown on over 15,000 acres in Oregon—the majority around Madras. This acreage complements that grown in California (the top-producing state); occasionally garlic bulbs must be grown in a more northerly state and at a higher elevation to maintain the vigor of the crop.

**One-third of the world's supply of horseradish is grown in the area around Malin** (southeast of Klamath Falls), and at nearby Tule Lake (across the line in California). Real Japanese wasabi is also grown on the Oregon coast around Tillamook and is sold in restaurants in the state, and even in New York City.

Hop Yard near Butteville

**Oregon is the leading state in the production and sale of prunes and plums, blackberries, loganberries, black raspberries, and various seed grasses**—such as bent grass, fescue, ryegrass, orchard grass, and bluegrasses. It produces virtually all of America's ryegrass seed.

Burlingham Seeds in Rickreall sells grass seeds for the turf used in golf courses and playing fields all over the world; the company has been in business for over a century. It claims the Willamette Valley has an ideal climate for seed production and that **sixty percent of the world's production comes from here**.

Hazelnut Orchard in Canby

**The Hood River Valley leads the world in production of Anjou pears and grows about half of the nation's winter pear crop.** In fact, pears are the largest tree-fruit crop produced in the state. The Medford area specializes in growing Comice pears (a very sweet variety).

Eastern Oregon's Umatilla Basin produces food crops that are ideally suited to the needs of various fast-food operators: potatoes for baked potatoes (used by

*Natural Resources and Agriculture*

Wendy's) and French fries (used by McDonald's), and red onions for sandwiches (used by Subway). It has the second highest yield per acre for potatoes (after WA).

### NURSERIES AND FLOWERS

**Oregon ranks second in the nursery trade**, producing a wide variety of flower bulbs and rhizomes—including irises, peonies, daffodils, tulips, lilies, and gladioli—for the national market. For a while, the area around Brookings was a major producer of lilies for the bulb industry.

The nursery trade is now the leading agricultural sector in Oregon. Ornamental horticulture is the state's largest agricultural commodity. Oregon has 1800 nurseries and greenhouses, with a product valued at over $800 million. Oregon nurseries also produce cut flowers, which are shipped to markets throughout the country, competing with flowers from South America.

Oregon is also one of the best places to see these species of flowers in the spring as they bloom in commercial fields, which are concentrated in the northern Willamette Valley, though they are also seen in the summer in eastern Oregon around Nyssa (e.g., zinnias).

Among the nationally recognized specialty growers here is **Schreiner's Iris Gardens,** just north of Salem. In business since 1925, **this is the nation's largest retail grower of irises**, with 200 acres devoted to growing, and ten acres for display gardens that are open to the public, with 500 varieties in bloom. Cooley's Garden is also a major grower of irises.

Swan Island Dahlias in Canby

"**Oregon is iris heaven**," proclaims a spokesman for the American Iris Society. "Where else can you see millions of irises in one place? There is nothing like it anywhere."

Adelman Peony Gardens is another esteemed specialty grower. Based in Brooks, the gardens feature 250 varieties of peonies on fifteen acres. The growers have been in the peony business for over twenty years, and have won "best in show" awards at the American Peony Society for seven out of the last ten years.

Swan Island Dahlias **is the nation's largest grower of dahlias**, and is located in Canby. Over 350 varieties are grown there on forty acres, with 400,000 tubers planted each year. Tubers are shipped all over the world.

Heirloom Roses, twenty-five miles south of Portland, is one of the state's highly regarded sellers of roses. Thousands of them are displayed on five acres of themed gardens.

The Willamette Valley is thought to have the **best climate for growing daffodils**. Over half a dozen growers in the state are highly regarded. Daffodils can be seen in season at the forty-acre Wooden Shoe Gardens, north of Salem; 117 varieties of tulips are grown there as well. These gardens have been in business since 1974.

In the spring, spectacular displays of wildflowers can also be seen at the east end of the Columbia Gorge, as around Mosier and Rowena Crest, where balsamroots paint the hillsides with yellow, daisy-like flowers. The spring wildflower show at Glide (seventeen miles east of Roseburg) is also famous for its diversity: over 300 native flowers from that vicinity are on display.

# CHAPTER 9

# SOCIAL MATTERS

## HEALTH

Oregon is **top ranked for reproductive health** (i.e., low rates of unintended pregnancies, high rates of sex education, emphasis on abstinence, and access to means of contraception). This ranking is by the Population Institute.

Oregon has **the lowest rate of premature births in the nation** (7.7 percent in 2015), earning an "A" rating from the March of Dimes.

Oregon has one of **the highest newborn breastfeeding rates in the country**. By six months of age, more babies are breastfed in Oregon than anywhere else.

Oregon is also among the states leading the way in educating parents to avoid shaking and injuring newborns when they cry hard for long periods.

The health of children in Oregon is ranked seventh in the nation overall, partly due to the following statistics:
- Most Oregon newborns have good birthweights
- The infant mortality rate is low
- Drugs and alcohol abuse by children is low
- Teenage pregnancy rates are low
- Most children (ninety-four percent) are insured

(Assessments of the health of children, though, do vary according to how many factors are considered.)

The rates of hunger in Oregon vary from year to year, according to how much funding Congress provides to the SNAP program (formerly known as the Food Stamp program). In a 2015 assessment, Oregon **was rated either outstanding or satisfactory in the feeding of poor students**. Sometimes Oregon's hunger rate is below the national average, and sometimes it is a bit above. In any event, all of these numbers are based on estimates.

As of 2010, **Oregon had the nation's lowest rate of childhood obesity** (though the overall rate has been creeping up in recent decades).

Oregon is third in terms of the amount of physical exercise its residents get.

Oregon has one of the nation's lowest rates of death from heart disease (it is in second place).

The school district in Salem has one of the most respected teams in the country for assessing the risk of gun violence by students. They are consulted widely.

The University of Oregon became the first Pac-12 institution to announce a policy of not allowing tobacco on its campus.

Oregon is among the eleven states whose family leave laws go beyond federal requirements. For quite some time, **Oregon has been a leader in enacting laws on family and medical leave. It passed the first one in 1987**, and expanded it in 1989, and again in 1991. This legislation **became the model for federal laws enacted in 1993**.

**Oregon is among the top states in providing support to people needing long-term care.**

An Oregon hospital (Providence, in the Portland area) had the fastest time (a critical factor) in removing blood clots from the brains of people experiencing a stroke. This was in a 2015 competition with thirty other hospitals from around the country.

Oregon was the state that in 1991 originated the POLST (physician orders for life-saving treatment) form to advise doctors treating life-threatening illnesses. It is a standard medical form telling doctors whether the patient wishes to have various heroic steps taken to sustain their lives. It is now used in twenty-six states.

*Social Matters*

Oregon was one of the first states to require that, when doctors do breast mammograms, they immediately tell the women tested of the density of their breasts and the danger of cancer developing in them.

**Over ninety percent of Oregonians now have health insurance**—a statistic that reflects gains made under the Affordable Care Act (ACA). According to the 2014 Census, the percentage of uninsured in the state is clearly below the national average (9.7 percent vs. 11.7 percent). In fact, a study by OHSU claimed it was even lower (5 percent). Whichever figure is true, Oregon is now one of only a handful of states having so few uninsured.

Oregon is also making strong efforts to control costs under the ACA. To do that, it is using Coordinated Care Organizations to control costs (while striving to maintain the quality of the care provided). Its unique program does this with regional teams of health-care providers.

### EDUCATION

The number of college-educated people in Oregon is slightly higher than the national average (28.6 percent vs. 27 percent).

In a recent year, Oregon high-school graduates met college readiness benchmarks at higher levels than the national averages, as reflected in ACT tests. This was the case in a number of subjects: mathematics (forty-nine percent to forty-six percent), science (thirty-five percent to thirty-one percent), and reading (fifty-five percent to fifty-two percent). In 2013, in math, science, and reading, ACT scores were about six points above the national average. **Between 2013 and 2015, the SAT scores of its students have also been above national levels in reading, writing, and math.**

Questions have been raised about Oregon's high school graduation rate. The rate is acceptable for children of parents of the dominant culture (that of urban Euro-Americans and Asian-Americans), while that of others tends not to be.[6] The parents of children of the dominant cultures stress the importance of school performance and graduation, which others sometimes do not. For various reasons, some students in Oregon take five years to complete high school. When this is taken into account, the rate of graduation from high school in Oregon is in line with the national average (at 82%).

While Oregon tends to spend less per student than the national average, the key thing is how well its students are educated. Test rankings suggest that they are being well-educated, even with a lower level of spending.

One should also note that spending per student varies widely among states and over time. And results do not always correlate with spending.

Moreover, in recent years, the Oregon legislature has appropriated record amounts for K-12 education. Oregon now outspends twenty other states in what it provides for these students (a figure comparable to Washington State, and exceeding California). Funding is now provided for a full day of kindergarten.

6 The only exception to this graduation rate for white children is in some rural, one-time timber communities, where jobs used to be readily obtained in the mills—even for those who did not complete high school.

## RELIGION

Oregon is now thought to practice a high level of religious tolerance.

While just under eighty percent of Oregonians list themselves as Christians, thirty-seven percent of Oregonians are not affiliated with any church. Forty-two percent of Portlanders are unaffiliated with any church—making it **the most religiously unaffiliated area in the country**. On a per capita basis, Benton County is the least religious county in the country. Overall, Oregon has the highest number of non-believers (seventeen percent).

Those who classify themselves as Protestants are split between many denominations. Only about one-third of the adherents of various Protestant denominations are thought to regularly attend services.

Thirty percent of Oregonians think of themselves as evangelical Christians; this is higher than the national average (which is twenty-six percent). Also compared with the national average, fewer people here see themselves as mainline Protestants (who have been losing adherents).

The most numerous Oregon denominations are the Roman Catholics (315,000), the Church of Latter Day Saints (130,000), and the Evangelical

Lutherans (49,000). The state also has the largest community of Russian Old Believers (10,000). Portland's First Unitarian Church has one of the largest congregations of that denomination in the country.

But while Catholics are only between ten and fourteen percent of the population in Oregon, they have the largest number of associated schools, hospitals, and colleges. Various orders of monks and sisters also have establishments in the state: a Benedictine Abbey (Mount Angel), a Trappist Abbey (Lafayette), a Brigittine Priory (Amity), and a Servite Monastery (Portland). Religious communities for Catholic women exist in Eugene (the Carmelites), Portland (the Franciscans), Beaverton (the Sisters of St. Mary of Oregon), and Mount Angel (the Benedictine Sisters). There seem to be more such institutions than their populations would warrant.

The Catholics and the Methodists were the first to establish churches in the state. However, at the time of settlement, Presbyterians and Methodists were the most influential in setting the tone and culture of the state; these groups were strong in the small towns that dominated the state.

The oldest continuously used Methodist church in Oregon was built in 1844 in Oregon City (the Oregon City United). The oldest still-standing Baptist church building west of the Rockies is the West Union Baptist Church in Hillsboro, built in the early 1850s. The oldest extant building of the Presbyterian Church in the Northwest (once the Pleasant Grove Presbyterian Church) is now part of the Mission Mill Museum in Salem.

## CHARITY

Oregon is **above the national average in terms of how much its residents give to charity** as a percentage of their income (2.16 percent vs. the national average of 2.1 percent). In 2012, it was the nineteenth most generous state.

Major world charities are based in Oregon: Mercy Corps, Medical Team International, and These Numbers Have Faces.

Food drives, such as **Stamp Out Hunger** (run by the National Association of Letter Carriers), **began in Eugene many decades ago**. It now operates in 10,000 communities across the nation, and has delivered over one billion pounds of food. It **is the largest food drive in the nation**.

Food for Lane County is one of the top-rated charities for providing food to the hungry. It is rated as a four-star charity by Charity Navigator—in the top class with only a few other such groups around the country.

Eugene is reputed to have more human-service organizations, on a per capita basis, than any other community. For instance, it is the headquarters of Holt International Children' Services.

## CRIME AND INCARCERATION

**The murder rate in Oregon is about half the average national rate.** And **the rate of violent crimes is also much lower than the national rate.**

**Oregon's rate of incarceration of convicted criminals is among the lowest third in the nation.**

*Social Matters*

# CHAPTER 10

# OREGON'S ROLE IN WARS

Since the Civil War, the citizens of Oregon have been involved in the nation's wars—often distinguishing themselves as soldiers. In addition, troops from elsewhere have been trained here.

## CIVIL WAR

During the Civil War, the task of protecting settlers in eastern Oregon was turned over to new units organized by the state government—the 1st Oregon Volunteer Cavalry Regiment and the 1st Oregon Volunteer Infantry. The formation of these troops permitted the regular Army units, which had done that work up until that time, to go east to fight in the Civil War. When the war was over, these protective duties were given back to the regular army.

Fears that the Confederacy might attack facilities at the mouth of the Columbia River triggered the construction of Fort Stevens, near Astoria.

**The only US senator killed as a soldier in the Civil War hailed from Oregon**: Senator/Colonel Edward Baker, who was killed on October 1861 at Ball's Bluff, fighting on behalf of the union. In fact, he was the only member of Congress to die in that war.

Corporal Louis Renninger, who won the Medal of Honor for his bravery in the Civil War, is buried in Eugene's Pioneer cemetery. He originally came from Ohio.

The westernmost violence related to the war occurred in Oregon in 1865, on the occasion of President Lincoln's assassination. Southern sympathizers in Lane County's Long Tom district threatened a rebellion. One of their leaders—Philip Mulkey—was arrested, but a pro-union mob broke him out of jail to try to lynch him. There was the threat of a knife fight. The first Oregon Volunteer Infantry took Mulkey into custody and shipped him to Fort Vancouver.

### SPANISH-AMERICAN WAR

During this war, Oregon's Second Voluntary Infantry Regiment was federalized (in 1898) and sent to the Pacific theater. It was among the first to land in Guam and accept its surrender; it was the first to land in the Philippines (on the island of Cavite) and quickly secured it; then it went on to secure the city of Manila, which, after a quiet surrender, was beset by an insurgency six months later. It took a long, hard campaign to put this insurgency down. Oregon's National Guard forces were proud of their many firsts in that war.

### WORLD WAR I

Oregon's National Guard unit was federalized early in this war and became the US Army's 41st Infantry Division. It was sent to Europe and was used as a replacement reserve. Nonetheless, elements of it did fight in major encounters: Aisne-Marne, Meuse-Argonne, Chateau-Thierry, and San Mihiel. It was proud of the fact that it was the first National Guard unit to be called upon, and the first to mobilize and report.

### INTER-WAR PERIOD

In between wars, Oregon's National Guard had some unusual units.

They included eight companies of Coast Artillery units, and three Naval Militia companies, including a Marine detachment. In 1938, its coast artillery contingent (having practiced at Fort Stevens) won a national trophy for proficiency, which was the first time a National Guard unit had won it. This was among the most complex of military operations.

### WORLD WAR II

In World War II, **Oregon was the part of the mainland to most directly experience hostilities from Japan**. Japan's submarines fired seventeen shells at Oregon's Fort Stevens. Twice Japanese submarines fired at oil tankers nearing the mouth of the Columbia River. One was sunk by a Japanese submarine off Port Orford. A light airplane from an I-25 submarine firebombed Mt. Emily in the Siskiyou National Forest and Cape Blanco. Six people were killed when an incendiary bomb from a Japanese balloon exploded in a southern Oregon forest near Bly. Another such bomb was detonated in Medford. Remnants of forty balloons of this sort have been found in eleven counties in Oregon. At the time, news of the prevalence of these balloons was suppressed.

The attack on Fort Stevens was the first on a continental US fortification in 130 years. And the fatalities at Bly were the only fatalities on the US mainland since the war with Mexico in 1848.

American fighter planes then regularly patrolled Oregon's coasts searching for enemy submarines to attack, and, later, Japanese balloons to shoot down. In 1942 and 1943, the Coast Guard had armed crews on horses, with trained dogs, patrolling Oregon's beaches. In time, blimps from Tillamook also searched for submarines. People living along the coast were obliged to black out their windows at night, with Block Wardens enforcing this practice; also at night, residents had to dim their car headlights.

The Army Air Corps had airfields at the Portland, Pendleton, Madras, Medford, Corvallis, and Salem airports. It also constructed airstrips at various spots along the coast: Astoria, Newport, North Bend, and Floras Lake (north of Port Orford). It used its airfields to conduct coastal patrols and train air crews. Some were also used to transport war materiel.

Naval aviators were based at the Tongue Point Naval Air Station (near Astoria) and at the Klamath Falls Naval Air Station. And of course, Navy blimps were stationed at Tillamook. At Boardman, there was a Naval Weapons Training Facility (1941). Nearby, at Hermiston, there was an Army Weapons Depot.

Up and down the Oregon coast, volunteer airplane spotters stationed in forest fire towers looked for enemy planes around the clock. News of each plane spotted was phoned in to filter centers in nearby cities, to see whether it was a plane that could be accounted for or not. These volunteers were all part of a system called the Aircraft Warning Service, with its Ground Observer Corps; there were over 100,000 of these spotters all along the West Coast.

People of Japanese ancestry in western Oregon were forcibly interned in the spring of 1942. This was part of a federal order to minimize the perceived risk of sabotage in a war zone along the West Coast. Up to 120,000 were interned in bleak camps in the interior—including 4000 from Oregon. This reflected a sense of anxiety over security in the zone: Pearl Harbor had been heavily bombed, Wake Island (US) and the Philippines (US) had been invaded, and US islands in Alaska (Attu and Kiska) were about to be. British Singapore was on the verge of falling, Thailand had fallen, and much of China had been taken.

These hostile actions made Americans along the West Coast nervous, even if later these internments would not seem to have been warranted, and indeed were an unjust way to treat the internees—many of whom were, after all, American citizens.

Oregon's National Guard force, the 41st Infantry Division, was federalized in 1940 in anticipation of hostilities. It was the **first American division to go overseas** after the declaration of war, **served longer overseas than any other division**, was the first trained for jungle warfare, **fought in more campaigns than any other**, and killed and captured more enemy in the Pacific theater than any other. It fought mainly in New Guinea and the Southern Philippines and was part of the "island-hopping" operation. In one campaign, it fought continuously for seventy-six days. That earned its soldiers the nickname "jungleers."

When the war was over, it was released from active federal duty and once again became the National Guard unit in Oregon. Known as the "Sunset Division," it trained at Camp Clatsop (now Camp Rilea) on the northern coast of Oregon.

Four other divisions were trained in Oregon during World War II—three at Camp Adair near Corvallis and one at Camp White near Medford. Engineering training also took place at Camp Abbott south of Bend (on the site of today's Sun River resort). The army units trained here were the 96th Infantry Division, which saw service in the Philippines and at Okinawa; the 104th Infantry Division, which saw service in France and Germany; the 91st Infantry Division, which saw service in Italy; and the 70th Infantry Division, which saw service in Germany's Saarland. After taking their share of casualties, all won various citations for bravery.

## CHAPTER 11

# HISTORIC PRESERVATION

Oregon has been vigorous in preserving structures of historic value, especially in Portland.

### HOTELS

Portland has preserved many of its fine hotels.

Its **Benson Hotel** has always been kept in first-class shape, having been built in 1912 by Simon Benson as a **"world-class hotel."** Originally called the "Oregon Hotel," it was added to the National Register in 1986.

The Multnomah/Embassy Suites Hotel (1912) was the largest hotel in the Northwest when it was built. It was added to the National Register in 1985, and restored in 1995.

When it was built, the **Heathman Hotel** (1927) was the state's largest construction project. It has always been an upscale hotel. It was renovated and added to the National Register in 1984. *Travel and Leisure* placed it **on their list of the World's Best Hotels** in 2005. It has also been recognized as an important historic hotel.

Many of Portland's oldest hotels have also been restored:
- The Imperial/Vintage Plaza Hotel (1894) was remodeled in 1991, after having been added to the National Register in 1985.
- The Imperial/Vintage Plaza's one-time companion, The New Imperial Hotel/Hotel Lucia (1909), has recently been renovated.

Michael McCloskey | 91

Oregon: A State That Stands Out

Mural on OHS Building

- Portland's historic Seward/Governor/Sentinel Hotel (1909) was restored in 1992, after having been added to the National Register in 1985.
- The Mallory/De Luxe Hotel (1912) was renovated in 2006 and added to the National Register that year.
- Portland's art-deco Commodore Hotel (1927) is now an apartment house. But it has been kept up and is on the National Register. (It should not be confused with the Commodore Hotel in Astoria, which has also been restored but is less significant as a structure.)
- The Sovereign Hotel (1923) was converted into apartments in 1938. While the Oregon Historical Society owned it, murals were painted on its side, celebrating Oregon history. It was added to the National Register in 1981.

### FAILURES

Despite these successes, however, Portland failed to save its most magnificent hotel—the Portland Hotel, opened in 1890, and initially financed by railroad magnate Henry Villard. With 362 rooms, it occupied a full block, and was built in Queen Anne style, in the manner of a chateau. It was designed by noted New York architect, Stanford White. Eleven US presidents stayed there.

It was torn down in 1951, before historic preservation came into vogue. Some of the wrought-iron panels from its entry court were preserved, and have been placed at the northeast corner of the plaza built on its site.

That plaza, called the Pioneer Courthouse Square, was built in the 1970s when citizens rebelled against plans for a two-story parking structure that the department store, Meier and Frank, wanted to build there. The city then acquired the site and went through an elaborate process to finance and design the square.

Portland also failed to save its cherished Congress Hotel (1912), which was demolished in 1977. For many years, it had attracted a clientele of important public figures. In some ways, it was the victim of the confusion of a long construction project for a new transit mall.

Bend also did not save its celebrated Pilot Butte Inn. Built in 1917, in Craftsman style (with batten-boards combined with quarried stones on its sides, and gabled roofs), it was a destination for fly fishermen headed toward the Deschutes River. It was also used by Hollywood stars and Eleanor Roosevelt. Though it was finally placed on the National Register in 1973, it was torn down in the same year.

But Baker City has saved and restored its impressive Victorian Geiser Grand Hotel (1889). (It has also saved its City Hall (1903), the St. Francis Cathedral (1908), and its Carnegie Library (1909). It uses a special historic district tax to finance its preservation work there.) And Astoria has done a fine job of restoring its old Elliott Hotel.

Old Portland Hotel

Pilot Butte Inn

## HISTORIC MOVIE THEATERS

The state is now also focused on preserving cherished movie theaters.

One of them is the Paramount Theater in Portland. It was built in 1927 and designed in Italian Renaissance style by Rapp and Rapp. At the time, it was considered to be a very large and lavish theater for a city of Portland's size. It seated nearly 3000, had dressing rooms for 90, and was decorated with crystal chandeliers and marble. The city made it a historic landmark in 1972. It was added to the National Register in 1976, and was

Oregon: A State That Stands Out

restored in 1983. It is now the Arlene Schnitzer Concert Hall, home of the Oregon Symphony and showcase for numerous other artists.

Astoria has also restored its Liberty Theater, built in 1925 in Romanesque style as a movie theater and vaudeville house. It is now an exquisite venue for live performances. Salem has also restored its stunning 1926 Elsinore Theater, thanks to strenuous citizen efforts (including fund-raising drives). This venue has the largest theater organ in the PNW.

In Portland, citizen efforts have also kept the Hollywood Theater going. Another impressive neighborhood theater there, the Bagdad, has been kept going by the McMenamin brothers. The latter was designed by architects Lee Arden Thomas and Albert Mercier.

As of this writing, similar preservation efforts are underway in:
- Albany (the Pix Theater, being restored)
- Ashland (the Varsity Theater, partially restored)
- Baker (Eltrym Theater, being restored)
- Bend (the Tower Theater, restored in 2002)
- Clatskanie (the Avalon Theater, now the Birkenfeld; restored in 2015)
- Coos Bay (the Egyptian Theater)
- Corvallis (the Whiteside Theater)
- Eugene (the McDonald Theater, being restored by the Kesey family)
- Forest Grove (the Forest Theater)
- Grants Pass (the Rogue Theater, restored in 2000)
- Hillsboro (the Venetian Theater, restored in 2008)
- Klamath Falls (the Esquire Theater, restored in 1989)
- La Grande (the Liberty Theater)
- Lincoln City (the Bijou Theater, formerly known as the Lakeside Theater)
- McMinnville (the Mack Theater, restoration contemplated)
- Medford (the Craterian, restored in 1997; the Holly is now being restored)
- Pendleton (Rivoli Theater, restoration beginning)
- Tillamook (Coliseum Theater, remodeling underway)

Portland Theater (Old Paramount Theater)

The Egyptian Theater in Coos Bay was added to the National Register in 2010, with the National Park Service finding that nationally it was one of only four still-intact theaters in this style. The Rogue Theater in Grants Pass was added to the National Register in 2005, and La Grande's Liberty Theater was added to the register in 2009. The 1922 Rivoli Theater in Pendleton is now being restored after having been threatened with demolition; a nonprofit acquired it.

The state agency, Travel Oregon, has given the University of Oregon a grant to catalogue the condition of historic downtown theaters in Oregon. These theaters are seen as assets in reviving the centers of these towns, employing hundreds of people and having $23 million in economic impact.

## OTHER COMMERCIAL BUILDINGS

Portland has also made progress in saving the beautiful downtown buildings that once housed its department stores. The Meier and Frank store (built between 1909 and 1915) was sold to Macy's, which has retained the lower five stories, while converting the higher ones into a hotel. Olds and King (1910) went out of business in 1974, but its building has been converted into the Galleria; it has had various tenants but has found a way to survive. Lipman-Wolfe (1912), near Meier and Frank, closed at this location in 1986, and its building has also been turned into a hotel (the Hotel Monaco). All of these buildings have been added to the National Register.

Other important commercial buildings have been kept going—consider the Charles F. Berg Building (1902), which housed an upscale women's wear store, and is still admired for its art deco exterior featuring gold inlays. It also was added to the National Register in 1983. The *Oregon Journal* building (1912; now known as the Jackson Tower building) was renovated in 1972, though it ceased being occupied by the *Journal* in 1948. It was added to the National Register in 1996.

Oregon: A State That Stands Out

**Portland also has one of the largest collections of cast-iron fronted buildings on the West Coast**—most of them in its urban core, near the river. Also known as the Skidmore Old Town Historic District, this area is a National Historic Landmark. Between 1854 and 1889, ninety percent of Portland's buildings were faced with cast iron. Most of that iron came from the iron works at Lake Oswego. Photographer Minor White documented these buildings in photographs for the WPA in the late 1930s, before many were lost.

The Barber Block on Southeast Grand Avenue dates from the same era—the 1890s. An eclectic building complex in a variety of styles (Victorian, Italianate, and Richardsonian), it has survived proposals to demolish it, and was renovated and added to the National Register in the late seventies. It is now the centerpiece of the Historic District.

Portland has its share of structures that are appreciated for their architecture. It has a number of bank temples (i.e., banks built in a very ornate, grand, classical style), such as the US Bank Main Branch Building, designed by A.E. Doyle. Built in 1917 and clad in imported marble with Corinthian columns, it continues to be used as a bank. It was modeled after New York's Knickerbocker Trust Bank (designed by McKim, Mead, and White). Doyle also designed scores of fine downtown office buildings in the 1920s.

Cast Iron Building Facade in Portland Skidmore District

### CIVIC BUILDINGS

Portland has also turned toward renovating many of its historic civic buildings, rather than replacing them with new ones. Its City Hall, built in 1895 and designed by Whidden and Lewis (who trained with the New York firm of McKim, Mead, and White), has been upgraded repeatedly over the years, and underwent a major overhaul in 1996-98. Designed in Italian Renaissance style, it was added to the National Register in 1974.

Portland City Hall

Portland's county Central Library underwent a major rehabilitation in 1994-97, having been constructed in 1913. Designed by A.E. Doyle, it is in American Renaissance style, with Georgian touches. It contains over 2 million books.

The city's neo-classical style Multnomah County Courthouse, built in 1909-1914, was also designed by Whidden and Lewis. It was added to the National Register in 1979. Regrettably, a tentative decision has been made to tear it down rather than to undertake an extensive renovation.

Barber Block on Grand Avenue in Portland

The future of the old US Customhouse in Portland is still being worked out. Built in 1897 and designed in Italian Renaissance style (with mannerist exterior detailing), it was once occupied by a series of federal agencies, which have since left. While it has undergone rehabilitation both inside and out (in 1977 and 1992, respectively), it still needs earthquake retrofits and modern accessibility. It was made a city landmark in 1970 and listed in the National Register in 1973. It was finally sold at a GSA public auction in 2012, to a firm that plans to rent rooms to start-up firms.

The Portland Federal Building, built in 1919, and later used as the main post office, has at last been renovated. It is currently serving as the headquarters for the Northwest College of Art.

The magisterial Gus Solomon United States Courthouse has been used for a variety of purposes. While constructed comparatively recently—in 1933—it has been on the National Register since 1979, and was renovated in 1984. A very formal building, it was designed in the Renaissance Revival style. Its interiors have been featured in various movies.

The Portland Art Museum is also a newer building, having been built in 1932 and expanded in 1939, with later additions in 1970. It was designed by Pietro Belluschi, in early modern style, and with classical proportions. It was added to the National Register in 1974. It has been renovated a number of times. The Masonic Temple next to it was acquired and added to the complex in 2005.

Other civic structures have been renovated too: Portland's Civic Sports Stadium (designed by A.E. Doyle), for instance, and its civic auditorium (now called the Keller Auditorium). Built in 1917, the Keller is used by the city's opera and ballet companies. As a building, however, it is not much loved, either for its architectural style or its acoustics.

A newer building that also has not been popular is the Portland Building, designed in 1982 in a post-modernist style by Michael Graves. It looks like a long box wrapped in ribbon. When it was built, it was celebrated as a possible forerunner of a new style. The *Portlandia* statue on its front side is popular, but Graves would not allow it to be moved to a different site where it could be more easily seen. The city staff who work there complain about the lack of windows and the leaks; and it needs seismic upgrades. The city is already pondering whether to renovate or remove it.

Portland's fine Union Train Station dates back to 1896 and was designed in Italian Renaissance style. Nationwide, **Portland's Union Station is the second oldest still in operation**. It has had minor renovations over the years. In other cities—such as Salem, Albany, Eugene, and Medford—the original train stations have also survived, and most are still in use. Other, smaller ones have survived too, though many are now used for other purposes.

The record demonstrates that, most often, Portland prefers to save its historic buildings, finding ways to accommodate changing needs by renovating them rather than tearing them down. Restore Oregon (formerly the Historic Preservation League of Oregon) promotes the maintenance of historic structures in the state, and publishes a list of endangered buildings. Portland citizens devoted to that cause have organized a center to promote it: the Architectural Heritage Center.

## OTHER BUILDINGS

The Ladd Carriage House (1883) has somehow survived in a changing environment. It was almost lost in 2007, threatened by an adjoining high rise, but preservationists worked out an arrangement that has saved it again. It has moved on and off the National Register, but currently is back on again. In 2000, Portland State University also saved the Simon Benson House by moving it and renovating it for its use; it has been on the National Register since 1983.

Portland has many admirable churches too. For instance, its Temple Beth Israel Synagogue, built in 1928 and designed by Herman Brookman, is considered to be one of the finest examples on the West Coast of the Byzantine style and was modeled on European examples. The city's oldest church, dating back to 1882 and still located on its original site, is the Calvary Presbyterian Church (also known as "The Old Church"). It was saved from demolition by a determined public campaign.

Ladd Carriage House

The city thought so highly of the Pittock Mansion, with its spectacular view of the Cascade peaks, that it bought the building even after it had been damaged in the Columbus Day Storm of 1962 and was subsequently threatened with demolition; it had been for sale since 1958. Built in French

*Historic Preservation*

Renaissance style, the Pittock Mansion has always been one of the great mansions of the city. It has now been restored and added to the National Register. A number of movies have been shot there.

Lloyd Frank Mansion in Portland

Another of the great mansions of the city is the Lloyd Frank Mansion (1924), with its eight acres of gardens framing a view of Mt. Hood. This building is now part of the Lewis & Clark campus. The Autzen House N.E. Alameda is also noteworthy. It was once owned by the man who invented plywood. Built in 1927 in Tudor style, it has steeply pitched slate roofs, with large chimneys and scores of gables. Its exterior is half-timbered and faced with brick and stone.

A home of the celebrated Oregon governor and senator, George Chamberlain, survives in the Irvington neighborhood. Chamberlain was offered a spot on the Democratic ticket in 1916 by President Woodrow Wilson, but instead chose to return to this inviting house, which was originally built in 1891. It is on the National Register.

Other large, notable mansions in period styles are the Kenneth Mackenzie House (1892, now the William Temple House), the Wilbur Reid House (1914, in "Greene and Greene" style), the Frank Cobb House (1917), the Cameron Squires House (1920), the Clarissa Inman House (1926), and the Ernest Haycox House (1940). Near Portland are the Ainsworth House (1855) in Oregon City, and the Theodore Wilcox House (1919, west of Portland).

**Portland's Ladd's Addition Historic District was named as one of "America's Great Places"** by the American Planning Association in 2009. It is one of the oldest planned residential districts in the West, marked by diagonal streets and parks.

### ELSEWHERE IN THE STATE

The Jacksonville Historic District preserves many of the buildings of this one-time small mining town. The village dates back to the middle of the nineteenth century, and still has over ninety brick and mortar buildings from that time. The Aurora community, near Canby, also retains many historic buildings: at least twenty-five of them. Aurora was once a utopian Christian colony of German immigrants, and was founded 1856.

The oldest building still in use in an Oregon college is Waller Hall (1864), on the campus of Willamette University. A few years later, a small denominational college was founded as Philomath College (1867). While that college did not survive, its main building still stands as the Benton County Historical Museum. The second-oldest college in Oregon is Pacific University in Forest Grove (chartered in 1854), which grew out of the Tualatin Academy, started by the Congregational Church in 1842. Old College Hall there is its oldest structure; construction on it was begun in 1851, making it older than Waller Hall.

Salem has a particularly good record in preserving many of its fine buildings, such as the Ladd and Bush Bank Building (1868), the Reed Opera House (1869-70), the Eldridge Building (1889), the Gray Building (1891), the Masonic Temple (1912), and the First National Bank Building (1926). And the house and garden of Elizabeth Lord and Edith Schryver have been added to the National Historic Register. Lord and Schryver created the first firm of landscape architects in the Northwest owned and operated by women. The grounds of the Deepwood Estate, also in Salem, display their work.

Eugene, Albany, and Medford also have active city programs for historic preservation.

Among the Eugene properties that have been put on the National Register are the Smeede Hotel (1885), the Shelton-McMurphey House (1888; a large Victorian house at the base of Skinner's Butte), the Palace Hotel (1903), the Quackenbush Hardware Building (1903), the McMorran and Washburne Building (1913), the Eugene Hotel (1925), the McDonald Theater (1925), various fraternity and sorority houses at the University of Oregon, and Johnson Hall there (1915).

Chamberlain House in Portland

Eugene has restored two of its oldest cemeteries: its 1859 Masonic Cemetery (featuring the Hope Abbey Mausoleum, designed by Ellis Lawrence) and its 1872 Pioneer Cemetery, with its Grand Army of the Republic plot containing the graves of fifty-one veterans of the Civil War, statues commemorating that war, and the grave of Louis Renninger, winner of the Medal of Honor in that war.

At the University of Oregon, the Jordan Schnitzer Art Museum building (formerly the Murray Warner Museum of Oriental Art), built in 1932, was designed by Ellis Lawrence. It is an impressive, formal work—well-known for its intricate, west-facing facade. It was renovated and expanded in 2005. Lawrence also designed other major campus buildings, such as Gerlinger Hall and the Knight Library. The Art Museum and the Knight Library are both National Register properties.

University of Oregon Art Museum (Jordan Schnitzer) West Facade

The oldest buildings on the University of Oregon campus are Deady Hall (1885) and Villard Hall (1886)—both in the style of the Second Empire. Both of them are still in use, having undergone various renovations over the years. Both are on the National Register of Historic Places. Villard Hall is named after railroad tycoon Henry Villard, whose sizeable donations enabled the university to survive its early financial crises.

On the Oregon State University campus, the imprint of the nationally acclaimed landscape architect, John Charles Olmstead, can still be seen in the layout of its campus quads (from 1909).

Albany has the most varied collection of historic structures. It has four historic districts, with over 700 historic buildings. The Monteith House (1851)

is worth seeing, as it dates back to pioneer days; the Moyer House (1881), in Brownsville, is an Italianate-style house that is also worth seeing.

The Bennett-Williams House, in The Dalles, dates from 1899 and is marvelously preserved. It was built for a judge of the Oregon State Supreme Court, and is a fine example of the Queen Anne style. Another fine example of the Queen Anne style is the Flavel House Mansion in Astoria, built in 1885. It was the home of wealthy Columbia River Bar Pilot, Captain George Flavel. Also notable as an example of the Queen Anne style is the Settlemier House (1892) in Woodburn; it is now a museum. One of the oldest hotels on the coast (1914) is the Cannon Beach Hotel, which is still in business. The quaint Sylvia Beach Hotel in Newport is also over a century old, and has been restored.

A fine home in the Italianate style, and dating to 1855, is the Barlow House, near Canby. It was built by the son of the man who built the Barlow Road around Mt. Hood. The access road running to the mansion used to be lined with black walnut trees—a few still survive. The trees were planted by William Barlow, who arrived as a pioneer hungry for walnuts. At great expense, he imported them from back East, and showed great restraint by planting most of them, rather than eating them immediately. His investment and patience soon paid off, as the trees thrived on the site.

On Sauvie Island, near Portland, the Howell-Bybee house dates back to 1858. It is now in a regional park. Sauvie Island is the largest island in a river setting in the US.

Among the most interesting of the National Register properties in Medford are the Wilkinson-Swem Building (1896), the Southern Pacific Railroad Passenger Station (1910), the Sparta Building (1911), and, in Jacksonville, the John Orth Building (1872) and the Jeremiah Nunan House (1892).

Settlemeir House in Woodburn

Bennett-Williams House in The Dalles

*Historic Preservation*

Oregon: A State That Stands Out

Columbia River Gorge Hotel in Hood River

In Ashland, the Ashland Springs Hotel, built in 1925 as the Lithia Springs Hotel, was restored in 1998. This nine-story hotel is the tallest building in the Rogue River Valley. Designed in art deco style, it has been on the National Register of Historic Places since 1978.

The Applegate House in Yoncalla dates from the 1850s, and has remained in the same family for longer than any other residence in Oregon. It is an elegant house, with classical revival influences, and was restored in the 1970s. It is one of the most authentic houses from the pioneer era.

In John Day (Grant County), a grocery and apothecary, catering to Chinese laborers and dating to 1866, has been preserved as a state museum. It is known as the Kam Wah Chung Museum. Designated as a National Historic Landmark, it features **one of the most complete collections of materials from the period of Chinese immigration to the American West.**

The Columbia Gorge Hotel is magnificently situated on a bluff overlooking the Columbia River, just west of the city of Hood River. Constructed in 1904 in California Mission style, it was restored in both 1979 and 2012. Simon Benson was an early owner who promoted the hotel to prominent people. Among such people who stayed there were Presidents Theodore Roosevelt and Calvin Coolidge; and actresses Shirley Temple, Jane Powell, and Myrna Loy.

At Crown Point in the Columbia Gorge, the Vista House was erected to orient new visitors traveling along the gorge highway; it was the inspiration of Samuel Lancaster, who designed the **Columbia Gorge Highway, the nation's first scenic highway**. Built in 1916 and designed in Art Nouveau-style by Edgar Lazarus, the Vista House was added to the National Register in 1974. In 2005, it was thoroughly renovated in order to deal with deterioration caused by the severe weather that is common at this exposed point.

At Crater Lake, the park's lodge was much admired, but the 1915 building was so damaged by severe winters that it had to be replaced. A better building, with the same exterior design, was built on the same site in 1994. The superintendent's residence, in Munson Valley at the park, is still in its original condition. It is admired as **one of the best examples of a rustic installation in a national park.**

The Chateau at the Oregon Caves National Monument is a rustic lodge which actually has **a creek running through its lobby**; it **may be singular in this respect**. Its Monterey-style furniture all dates from the 1930s. The lodge

*Historic Preservation*

was restored in 2014, after being added to the National Register in 1992. The shaggy Port Orford cedar bark on its exterior is replaced as necessary.

Continuous efforts are underway to renovate the classic Timberline Lodge at Mt. Hood. It is considered to be **among the best examples of rustic mountain lodge architecture**.

**Henry Steiner's rustic cabins**, built in the Zigzag area between Government Camp and Brightwood, **are distinctive to Oregon**. Between 1928 and 1953, Steiner built almost a hundred of these structures by hand, using many twisted joints and bentwood to achieve a kind of folk-style log cabin that typically featured an arched entryway. Half have survived.

Chateau at The Oregon Caves Nat. Monument

In Baker County, one of the few remaining narrow-gauge, steam-powered railroads is still operating as the Sumpter Valley Railroad. Started in 1890 as a logging railroad, since 1976 five of its twenty-two miles have been restored. The railroad caters to tourists in the summertime. Much of its rolling stock was acquired from the White Pass and Yukon Railroad and from the Denver and Rio Grande Western. It has been added to the National Register.

Superintendent's House at Crater Lake Nat. Park

## CHAPTER 12

# SAFE DRIVING AND CAR DATA

Oregon is **one of the top two states in the degree of use of seat belts by its drivers** (as required by law).

Oregon is **one of the few states where you do not have to pump your own gas**—and it may soon be the only one.

Traffic fatalities in Oregon are now below the national average (as of 2014). Oregon was **the first state to keep track of this kind of fatality**, beginning in 1936. Eugene drivers are among the nation's safest; collisions occur less frequently there than in most places.

In 1919, Oregon became **the first state to levy a gas tax in order to raise funds to pave its roads**. (The focus then was on getting Oregon "out of the mud.")

In 1974, when gasoline was in short supply, Oregon developed a model that would later be used by many states to ration gasoline; it was done according to whether one's license plate ended in an odd or even number. One could only get gas on days designated for your type of number.

At one time, newcomers to the state were surprised at how courteous Oregon drivers were. As fewer drivers in the state now are native Oregonians, that trait may be diminishing.

Oregon is **the least expensive state in which to own a car**—considering the cost of repairs, insurance, gasoline, and taxes and fees (as of 2013).

Eugene was **the first city in the nation to implement one-way streets** as a way to reduce congestion.

Oregon's transportation department (ODOT) is well-known for being able to bring highway construction projects in under budget. Since 2003, it has brought 800 projects (in the aggregate) in at one percent under budget.

## CHAPTER 13

# BUSINESS AND THE ECONOMY

### A PLACE TO DO BUSINESS

In its 2016 evaluation of the economies of the various states, Bloomberg found **Oregon to have the best performing economy**, taking into account these factors: the employment rate, home prices, personal income, tax revenues, the mortgage delinquency rate, and how the equities of firms based in the state were faring. North Carolina and Michigan were next, but not close.

In 2012, one survey rated Oregon as **the best state for manufacturing**.

Oregon **leads the nation in the relative size of its manufacturing sector**, which is about fifteen percent larger than the national average for states. Portland has also retained more of its manufacturing base (as a percentage of total employment) than comparable cities.

Oregon leads the nation in manufacturing output per capita (a figure driven largely by its computer industry).

Oregon is among the top states in its exports of technology products (it is actually ranked seventh). Oregon is among the top ten states in trade per capita. It is the second highest in terms of exports as a share of the state's GDP.

Oregon is **one of two states with the highest number of patents per employee** (the other is Washington, and California is not far behind).

In an academic study, Oregon was noted as one of the top ten states doing the most to encourage entrepreneurship (measured in terms of the rate at which

Michael McCloskey | 109

businesses are formed, their growth, their number of patents, and income for the proprietors). In 2015, ***Forbes* magazine named Portland one of America's best cities for business** and career opportunities.

By 2011, Oregon's economy was making the second-fastest recovery from the 2008 recession. The *Bloomberg Oregonian Stock Index* for 2012 finished at 14 percent above the *Standard and Poor Index*. And jobs in the metro areas have grown faster than the national average.

Oregon has **ranked second in GDP growth per capita since 2007**—five times the national average. In the last quarter of 2013, Oregon's economy grew at 2.1 percent, in comparison to .8 percent for the nation (this is for hiring, unemployment rates, total wages paid, and manufacturing hours worked). Only two states exceeded this rate (Michigan and South Carolina).

**The rate of workmen's compensation levied against employers in Oregon is one of the lowest in the nation** (the state is in ninth place), but the level of benefits paid to employees (as of 2015) has been maintained.

Personal income has been growing rapidly in Oregon—in 2014, the growth rate was 4.6 percent. In recent years, Oregon has had **one of the fastest rates of growth in personal income**.

While the actual amounts of income earned in Oregon are a bit less than the national average, this is because more Oregonians work part-time, and because of a shorter average work week in the state. Oregon workers are thought to be willing to settle for less because of the importance they place on quality of life. Moreover, the cost of living in the state is lower in many places there. Klamath Falls, for instance, has been rated as among the least expensive places in the country to live.

In recent years, Oregon has been **ranked among the states having the lowest taxes**; this is calculated in terms of total taxes paid per $1000 of personal income (found in a Wisconsin study in 2006-07). As a percentage of capital invested in new jobs, Oregon has the second-lowest effective tax rate. **In terms of taxes on business,** the Council of State Taxation has found that **Oregon has**

**the lowest rates in the country.** And of the states with taxes on personal income, Oregon's tax revenue is less volatile than most.

A 2011 study by the Council on State Taxation rated Oregon as among the top five states with the "least regressive tax systems."

**The average effective tax rate of property taxes in Oregon is below the national average.** In 2015, it was 1.18 percent, in contrast to the national average of 1.29 percent.

But the volume of taxes collected in Oregon has been growing. Since the recession year of 2009, tax collections in the state have grown by over eleven percent—placing **Oregon among the top ten states in the growth of taxes collected.**

In terms of venture capital invested on a per capita basis, Oregon recently ranked in the upper third, which was up from prior years. In 2014, the investment of venture capital in Oregon businesses grew at the rate of 80 percent, in contrast to the national average of 50 percent.

Springfield has one of the lowest operating costs among cities on the West Coast, and is listed as among the twenty-five places in the country with the best logistics for businesses.

## WORKER WELL-BEING

**More workers join unions in Oregon than they do nationally** (17 vs. 11.8 percent), and Oregon is among the top ten states in the percentage of public employees who join unions. Employers in Oregon cannot punish workers who discuss pay rates in the workplace (an issue of concern to unions).

Oregon has **one of the highest minimum wages** (currently set to rise to $14.75 per hour by 2022 in the most populous counties). It has been higher than the federal minimum wage since the early 1990s. It is also **indexed to keep up with inflation**.

In 2015, the unemployment rate in Oregon was sometimes below the national average and sometimes above; now it is under 5%. But Oregon remains **among the top states in terms of job growth**.

The rate of poverty in Oregon is about average for the nation—sometimes a little below and sometimes a little above. Different sources have different estimates.

In Oregon, **employers must grant up to five days of paid sick leave** to each employee every year (applies to firms employing ten or more workers). It is **one of four states requiring this**.

Oregon is the only state requiring most employers to grant two weeks of bereavement leave to employees who have lost a family member. It also grants a period of leave to parents on the birth of a child. In recent decades, it has been a leader in enacting such legislation.

In Oregon, the workplace mortality rate has declined appreciably in recent years; it is now below the national average (2.9 per 100,000 in Oregon, versus 3.3 per 100,000 nationally).

Oregon is **among the top states in the earnings record of its public pension system** (PERS). In 2013, it was reported that Oregon delivered **the best returns measured on a one, three, and ten-year basis**.

### BUSINESS HISTORY

In 1880 Oregon **had the nation's largest salmon pack at Astoria**. In fact, it was called the "fishing capital of the world," with thirty-nine salmon canneries along the lower Columbia River.

The first salmon cannery in the PNW was established at St. Helens in 1834. From the 1850s on, barrels of salted salmon were shipped from Astoria, and ports along the Columbia, to destinations all over the world.

Until the 1930s, salmon were caught on Oregon beaches by teams of horses pulling purse seines—Oregon is one of the few places in which this practice was common. It was outlawed in 1948—allegedly as posing unfair competition to gillnetters. Fish-wheels had been outlawed earlier (in 1926) for the same reason.

In 1896, disgruntled commercial fishermen in Astoria—Finnish immigrants—struck the canneries when they felt the prices offered for their salmon were too low. All were members of the Columbia River Fisherman's Protective

Union. When the commercial canneries refused to yield, the union organized its own cooperative cannery, which became the leading brand on the Northwest Coast for the next fifty years. They were sold under two labels: "Cooperators Best" and "Gillnetters Best" [sic].

In 1897, the 20 Mule Team Borax company began exploiting borax deposits in the Alvord Desert—removing 10,000 pounds a day—and continued doing so for a decade.

In 1901, the city of Shaniko, in eastern Oregon, **was the world's top center for shipping wool**. In 1915, the largest sheep ranch in Oregon (the Imperial Ranch—a 70,000 acre ranch sixty miles north of Bend) was also one of the largest in the West. Its current owners emphasize sustainability.

As of 1905, the largest flourmill on the West Coast was in Portland.

In later decades of the twentieth century, Oregon produced more timber than any state; various places there were considered contenders for "**timber capital of the world**."

For quite a time, Coos Bay was the world's largest timber-shipping port.

**Plywood was developed by a University of Oregon graduate, Thomas Autzen,** as a product of his Portland Manufacturing Company. He developed a three-ply veneer of Douglas fir. He promoted it at the Lewis and Clark Exposition and sold it for use in making doors, as well as various other construction uses. Over time he developed a worldwide market for the material.

During World War II, Portland set the record for most productive shipyards. Kaiser Shipyards built ships at three sites around Portland (two within city limits), along with three other firms. Kaiser Shipyards built the *Joseph N. Teal* in just ten days—a production record at the time. These yards built over 1000 ships—mostly "Liberty Ships" (441 feet long), but some slightly larger "Victory Ships" (455 feet long). Portland was called "**the Liberty Ship Capital of the United States**."

Portland's shipyards were part of one of the biggest emergency shipbuilding complexes at that time—known as the Oregon Shipbuilding Corporation.

Oregon: A State That Stands Out

White Stag Sign in Portland

100,000 people worked there. 12,000 were women, who worked as welders and mechanics; most of the rest were blacks.

In World War I, the federal government contracted with shipbuilders, who employed over 30,000 workers in a number of Oregon ports (Portland, Astoria, Tillamook, and Marshfield) to produce wooden and steel ships. These were produced for the Emergency Fleet Corporation. The firm of Kruse and Banks, based in Coos Bay, also produced minesweepers.

During that same war, the military also took over the production of spruce for aircraft—producing fifty-four million board feet in Coquille and Toledo, as well as in Washington State. This was done under the auspices of the Spruce Production Board.

Portland's White Stag company was the first to manufacture and sell outerwear for skiing ("ski togs") to a national clientele. In the 1950s, it was the **largest producer of ski clothing in the country**. In the mid-1960s, it was acquired nationally and became obscure in the marketplace.

In the period of between 1920 and 1960, the brand of Jantzen women's swimwear of Portland enjoyed great success. In the 1920s, its advertising promoted "clean water." Its advertising also featured an internationally recognized logo. Experts have suggested that **its "red diving girl" logo** has been one of **the longest-lived of all logos in advertising history** (especially in the apparel industry). While the brand, started in 1913 by the Portland Knitting Company, was bought in 1980, the business continues.

The Meier and Frank department store in Portland, Oregon operated under that name between 1857 and 1966 (with the name finally disappearing in 2005). By about 1900, it had emerged as "one of America's great stores." It initiated many merchandising firsts: the first "money-back guarantees," the first home deliveries on any merchandise. For a while during the early 1930s, it was **the largest retail outlet west of the Mississippi**, and one of the largest stores in the US. During World War II, it promoted more war bond sales than any store. It was acquired by Macy's in 2000, as department stores went into decline.

Constructed in 1960, the Lloyd Center once claimed **to be the largest mall in the country** (for a while, it was definitely the largest in the Pacific Northwest). It was located not far from Portland's business district, rather than in the suburbs (as later became the practice with malls). Interestingly, the Lloyd Center played a role in clarifying free speech rights, as the site prompted two legal cases—one that went to the US Supreme Court (407 US 551) and one that went to the Oregon Supreme Court (307 Or. 674). These cases held that public protestors had a right to distribute their material on the grounds of the Center.

Woodburn's mall, for premium store outlets, now draws over 4.5 million visitors annually, and is **the most visited outlet mall on the West Coast**.

## LARGEST OR BEST OF ITS KIND

Portland's harbor has been **the nation's largest wheat export hub**—and the third largest in the world. It also has been the nation's third largest gateway for auto imports. Portland has been regarded as **the second most active center on the West Coast for hauling and distributing freight**. At the moment, the port is adjusting to a change in shipping lines coming to the port.

Between 2013 and 2015, Portland International Airport was ranked as the "**best US airport**" by both *Conde Nast* and *Travel and Leisure*. Zagat's Survey said it was the best of the thirty US airports it examined.

Among mainland airports, Portland has the best on-time departure record (a finding of statistician Nate Silver). It is also the favorite airport of the Air Line Pilots Association. On a worldwide basis, it has often been among the ten airports most favored for shopping. And now it **leads the trend toward featuring fine food for travelers**.

Grain Elevators on Portland Waterfront

Oregon has **the largest clutch of top-rated golf courses in the country**: Pacific Dunes, Bandon Dunes, Old Macdonald, and Bandon Trails—all near the city of Bandon. Golf courses around Bend have also been rated as among the twenty best places in the world for golf. Centennial Golf Course, near Medford, has been rated among the top public golf courses in the country. The Tokatee Golf Club, east of Eugene, has often been listed as among the top twenty-five courses in the country.

People have been moving to Portland in record numbers over the last quarter century (as reported by moving firms). In 2013 and 2014, it was the **top relocation destination in the US**.

Portland has one of the largest percentages of glazed terra cotta commercial buildings in its downtown. Thirteen are by architect A.E. Doyle, and stem from the era of quick growth between 1905 and 1930. The front along SW Alder (consisting of several buildings) has been called the famed "Wall of White."

For the first half of the twentieth century, a Portland man, Jim Walker, was the most prominent national figure in the model airplane kit business, selling 232 million kits.

In the 1980s, Umpqua Feather Merchants, in Roseburg, became the largest wholesaler of fishing flies and fly-tying materials in the country. Dennis Black was the proprietor.

The maps produced by Raven Maps in Medford have been called the **"most beautiful maps" made in America** by the *New York Times* and the *Wall Street Journal*.

A-dec, founded in 1964 in Newberg, is **the world's largest producer of dental equipment**. They started with dental chairs, and now produce a wide variety of equipment for dentists.

Powell's Books in Portland is **the world's largest bookstore**. At its various locations in Portland, it offers over 1.5 million books, both new and used.

Wieden + Kennedy in Portland is **one of the largest independently-owned advertising agencies**. Founded in 1980, it has been Nike's agency since that time. It has **been called "the most-awarded agency in the world"**—even winning Emmy awards. It has twice been dubbed "the agency of the year" by *Adweek* (in 2010 and 2012).

The Portland area now **has the nation's foremost concentration of companies selling to the outdoor recreation and athletic shoe market** by designing, producing, and selling athletic shoes, as well as outerwear. Over 700 firms of this type are now found here, employing some 14,000 people. Another 3200 people are self-employed in this business.

In October 2014, the business section of the *Oregonian* reported that the "Portland area has the highest concentration of footwear distribution and footwear manufacturing in the United States." It also noted that the Portland area is "**the worldwide leader for sports-product innovation, education, and research**."

Oregon hosts the headquarters for **Nike**, which is **the world's leading producer of athletic shoes and sporting goods**. It passed Adidas to attain that position in the 1980s, and fended off Reebok soon thereafter. The company employs as many as 8000 people in the state.

**Nike earns more sportswear and related patents each year than any other company.** In addition, other leading firms in Oregon are Adidas and Columbia. Keen, Under Armour, Woolrich Footwear, and Mizuno Sports Equipment have all opened offices here too. Now Oregon is being described "**as the global epicenter for athletic apparel**."

Nike Headquarters in Beaverton

Oregon has at least two world-class boot makers: the line of Danner boots for troops, loggers, climbing, and recreation, and the West Coast Shoe Company in Scappoose, which manufactures rugged work boots for loggers. The latter is one of the few remaining US firms still making custom boots from US products. It has been in business since 1918. Danner has been in business in Oregon since 1936.

Portland has attracted an unusually large collection of firms manufacturing and selling hunting and military knives. Some of the best-known are Benchmade, Coast Cutlery, Gerber, Kershaw, and Leatherman (which also sells a unique multi-tool).

Oregon also hosts a collection of companies making outdoor products: Antigravity Equipment in Portland makes mountaineering equipment. Yakima in Beaverton makes a variety of products, such as paddleboards; the original Yakima (a maker of cargo racks for vehicles) has now moved its operations to the Portland area as well. Burley in Eugene makes a bike-cargo trailer; Sunday Afternoon in Talent makes various types of headgear; and Snow Peak in Portland makes stoves for backpackers.

There are more than sixty firms in Oregon producing outdoor equipment.

### WELL-KNOWN BUSINESSES

Leupold & Stevens has been in business in Oregon for over a century, producing and selling surveying equipment, binoculars, scopes for rifles, and quality optics to a national market. In recent years, the company acquired Redfield Optics. It sells extensively to the US military, as well as the Secret Service.

**Seventy percent of the market for freeze-dried foods is supplied by the Mountain House firm** in Albany. Its products are used primarily by backpackers, but also by the military.

The oldest restaurant in the Northwest is Huber's Cafe in Portland, Oregon, started in 1879. Dan and Louis' Oyster Bar in Portland dates back to 1907.

The McCormick & Schmick's restaurant chain was started in Portland, OR. It grew out of the old Jake's Famous Crawfish House restaurant there—itself 110 years old (and one of the top ten seafood restaurants in the country). There **are now almost 100 restaurants in the chain across North America**—each with a classic "men's club" atmosphere (very conservative, with a nineteenth-century London style of décor).

In 1985, Portland's McMenamin brothers came up with a successful formula for restoring old sites—decorating them with whimsical painted interiors and converting them into brewpubs. There are now sixty-five establishments in the McMenamins chain. Many are interesting historical properties—nine are on the National Register. The McMenamins are credited with **making brewpubs a mainstream concept**, and now Portland has fifty of them—**more than any other city in the country**. In 2014, Portland was voted as the best US city for beer.

John Helmer's haberdashery in Portland is nationally known and has been in business since 1932; it features a fine selection of men's hats.

Dayna Pinkham in Portland has been **celebrated as one of the world's top milliners**. She sells to a worldwide clientele, including those buying ladies' hats for the Royal Ascot and the Kentucky Derby. Actresses and ambassadors are also among her clientele. Movie stars also buy handmade western hats from the Montana Peak Hat Company in Pendleton.

Klindt's in The Dalles is the longest-operating bookstore west of the Mississippi River. It was founded in 1870, and has been at the same location since 1893.

Hamley & Co. in Pendleton is known for producing "the finest hand-made saddles that money can buy." It has been in business for over a century. The Huston Custom Saddle Shop in Baker City is known for producing some of the softest saddles in the west. It has been in business for over forty years.

The Pendleton Woolen Mills of Oregon (whose main mill is in Pendleton) is one of the most long-lived and successful businesses in the state. It was founded in 1909 and is still operating under the ownership and guidance of the Bishop family. It has developed a unique product line, with trade blankets featuring Indian designs (the "Beaver State" and "Cayuse" blankets), plaid, woolen men's shirts, and other outerwear sold all over the country.

For much of the twentieth century, Harry & David in Medford has been a nationally important firm in the specialty food and gift mail-order catalogue business, promoting Comice pears and other premier fruits. It was once an innovator in that business, with its "fruit of the month" promotion. It is currently facing problems adjusting to changes in the market.

*Business and the Economy*

Bob's Red Mill, in Milwaukie, has established a unique business featuring stone-ground, whole-grain foods. Its steel-cut oats product won the 2009 world championship in Scotland for the best porridge. It advertises itself as "the world's premier natural, whole-grain food supplier." The mill is owned by its employees.

Rejuvenation in Portland has since 1977 reproduced lighting, doorknobs, and other hardware from classic periods. In the beginning it catered to remodelers, but then moved into producing a catalogue for a national market. Enjoying great success, Rejuvenation now receives coverage in dozens of national magazines. (Its work has been featured in such magazines as *Better Homes and Gardens, House Beautiful, Old House Journal, This Old House, Old House Interiors, Sunset, Women's Day,* and *Easy Designing*).

Neil Kelly Remodeling in Portland has built a growing business since it was started in 1947 by Kelly's father. With over 30,000 jobs under its belt, it has won scores of awards over the years (including some national ones). It has become noted for both the quality of its work and its imagination. In 2008, it was designated as the national remodeler of the year.

Portland has a number of award-winning architectural firms. The largest is ZGF, which is also **the fourth-largest in the country**. Founded in 1942, the firm now has five offices around the country—the largest is in Portland, where 250 people work. ZGF won the American Institute of Architecture's Firm Award in 1991, for consistently producing distinguished architecture. It is designing the new Homeland Security Department office in Washington, D.C. In Portland, it has designed many buildings, including the Convention Center, the KOIN center, and Doernbecher hospital.

The SERA architectural firm in Portland is proud of adhering to various environmental codes. It has adopted the Natural Step principles of sustainability and strives to achieve LEED designations for its buildings. It was third on *Architect Magazine*'s list of the fifty most sustainable architectural firms in the country. It is also owned entirely by its employees. It specializes in renovating historic buildings and urban infill. It renovated Portland's historic City Hall, and did the Nine's Hotel in the old Meier & Frank department store.

The Soderstrom firm, founded in 1984, also emphasizes sustainable design and gaining LEED designations for its buildings. It designed the largest solar-powered school west of the Rockies. It is headquartered in Portland and focuses on West Coast clients.

## FIRMS SUPPORTING AVIATION

Did you know that Oregon had an aviation industry? The firms discussed below provide components to that industry, as well as services.

Oregon has a number of firms that manufacture products for the aviation industry. For instance, **Boeing has its largest manufacturing plant in Gresham**, where it produces structures for wings, engine mounts, and flight controls. Boeing also has subsidiaries in the Columbia Gorge that produce unmanned aircraft (drones)—including Hood Tech in Hood River. A company in McMinnville also is now beginning to produce drones: Honey Comb.

The federal government has set aside three Oregon ranges to test drones: near Pendleton, at Warm Springs, and near Tillamook (areas with different climates). Researchers test the use of drones in search and rescue efforts, fighting fires, and agriculture.

A number of companies in Oregon produce helicopters for various purposes, including use as air cranes. Erickson bought the patent for Sikorsky S-64 helicopters, and produces and sells them worldwide. The twenty of these that it owns are used in fighting fires and in construction. Erickson has a local competitor, Columbia (based in Aurora), which uses (and hopes to produce) Boeing's CH-47 Chinook and C-46 Sea Knight helicopters. They do heavy-lifting work all over the world. A firm in Grants Pass, Carson Helicopters, has also modified Sikorsky helicopters (S-61s), which it uses for heavy lifting (as in logging) and firefighting.

LEKTRO in Warrenton has been providing electric tow tugs for aircraft since the 1980s. It has sold over 3000 of these to the airline industry. The company has been growing rapidly.

EPIC Aviation in Salem operates a fuel supply firm that serves 300 airports at locations across the US and Canada. Started in 1939, it supplies aviation gas and jet fuel, and has major contracts with the Defense Department.

Garmin AT operates a 150,000 square foot manufacturing plant in Salem that produces navigation and communication equipment for the aviation industry. It is a subsidiary of Garmin Ltd. of Switzerland, which produces aids to satellite navigation.

The Composites Universal Group in Scappoose sells advanced composites to firms for use in the fields of aviation, aerospace, transportation, and energy. It uses carbon fiber, fiberglass, and other composites which have the advantages of low weight and high strength.

Until recently, Evergreen Aviation—in McMinnville, OR—has operated a diverse group of aviation companies, including an international cargo airline with a fleet of Boeing 747s, and ground services at thirty-five US airports. The cargo fleet worked for the US government, including the Army and the CIA, by airlifting military equipment into warzones in Vietnam, Iraq, Kosovo, Kuwait, and Afghanistan. With US military operations in the Middle East now winding down, the call for its services has declined, pushing the firm into bankruptcy. At its peak, it operated a fleet of over 200 aircraft, and was one of the largest airfreight cargo companies in the world.

At the Hillsboro Airport, Hillsboro Aviation operates one of the largest combined flight-training schools—meaning students can learn how to fly both airplanes and helicopters—in the country. On the West Coast, it is the largest. It also sells parts for overhauls and runs a charter business.

A light aircraft industry is now beginning to develop in Bend. It is focused on designing and building personal aircraft from composites, which are cheaper to operate and easier to fly. Its largest firm, Columbia Aircraft, has just been bought by Cessna, which plans to expand operations in Oregon.

**Metals and Heavy Industry** (firms also involved in the aircraft industry are marked with an *)

Did you realize that Oregon has businesses involved in heavy industry and producing exotic metals?

*Wah Chang in Albany has been one of the country's largest producers of zirconium, titanium, and rare-earth metals. A Chinese mining engineer, Dr. K. C. Li moved to Albany in 1956. He was invited by the Bureau of Mines, which had a facility there, to produce high quality zirconium for the Navy's nuclear program. His plant also partnered with Boeing to produce niobium for rocket engines and satellites, as well as for nuclear power plants. By 1967, it had **become the world's largest producer of zirconium and other rare-earth metals**, gaining a virtual monopoly on the industry outside the Soviet bloc.

This booming business slumped with the end of the Cold War, when the demand for titanium dropped sharply. The slump was compounded by problems in the aircraft industry. This led Wah Chang to merge with other companies in the field (e.g., Allegheny Teledyne).

But in recent years, the company has reinvented itself, pursuing markets in the health industry, producing prosthetic hip and knee joints.

*Precision Castparts Corp. in Portland, Oregon is **a world leader in producing large complex castings for the aircraft business**, including various components of jet engines and airframes. It sells to Boeing, General Electric, and Pratt & Whitney. It also sells to the power industry and has 30,000 employees in worldwide operations (ten percent in Oregon). Precision Castparts is now Oregon's second-biggest business.

Through a recent acquisition, Precision Castparts is now the largest independent producer of titanium, which is used in manufacturing aircraft parts. It has two other acquisitions as well: Aerospace Dynamics International (which machines complex aircraft parts and contributes to commercial aircraft platforms )and aerospace manufacturer Noranco. Nationally, these businesses may generate a significant amount of toxic pollutants.

*ATI Pacific Cast Technologies in Albany produces complex cast titanium parts for aircraft and aerospace programs. Its parts are used in components of turbine engines, airframes, and launch vehicles. It sells to both military and commercial markets.

*The ESCO Corporation is a major manufacturing company headquartered in Portland, but with operations in twenty-eight sites around the world. Having been in business since 1913, it manufactures engineered metal wear parts for a variety of industries—such as mining, power, construction, forestry, and aerospace. Its products go into nozzles, blades, gas turbines, excavators, graders, and backhoes. It has recently been announced it is closing its plant at the Portland site, which is now too near a residential area.

*Oregon Iron Works, founded in 1944, is really a sophisticated fabricator of diverse components, starting with bridge structures and then moving into components for hydroelectric facilities. In the eighties, it began manufacturing small vessels for the US Defense Department (particularly the Special Forces). Then it moved into unmanned vehicles and designed small seaplanes built with composites. It then produced components for space launch towers and platforms for the US Ground-Based Missile Defense Program. It is now producing buoys for an experimental wave-energy system being pioneered at Oregon State University. It also has a subsidiary, United Street Car, which has a license to build streetcars from Skoda of the Czech Republic.

Schnitzer Steel of Oregon is **one of the nation's largest recyclers of scrap metal**; it also manufactures finished steel products. It handles both ferrous and non-ferrous metals, and ships out of six deep-water ports. Its steel plant in McMinnville uses electric arc furnaces, operating under the name of Cascade Steel. It ships scrap metal all over the world, particularly to emerging markets. Another recycler of metals is EG Metals in Hillsboro, which collects materials from across the country and ships to international markets. It also recycles discarded electronic devices.

Consolidated Freightliner started manufacturing heavy-duty trucks in Portland at Swan Island in 1949. After ending its relationship with Consolidated Freightways and later White Trucks, this operation became a free-standing firm in 1974. Its trucks sold well in the West because of sufficient power for steep western grades, as well as better access to the engine. Its trucks also afforded easier access to the cab, as well as a smoother ride.

In 1981, Consolidated Freightliner became a division of Daimler-Benz of Germany, and other related firms were acquired too. In 2000, Western Star Trucks was acquired, which was a Canadian successor of White Trucks.

The firm has since experienced ups and downs with varying market conditions, but the parent company has kept the Portland plant in operation, as has concentrated on products for the military market and on Western Star Trucks. Consolidated Freightliner is now the brand name for a wide range of truck products produced at various plants, including Portland. The parent firm is a leading producer of trucks. Portland is the North American headquarters of its truck division, Daimler AG.

The Greenbrier Company, based in Lake Oswego, is involved in the heavy-duty transport business. It began to produce railcars in 1958 and has since come to produce a wide variety of rolling rail stock, including tank cars (starting in 2008). It is now a leading producer of railcars, having manufactured over 11,000 at its plant in Clackamas County. In a recent year, it received orders to build 39,000 more railcars. It has acquired other plants to enable it **to build railcars around the country and the world**. It also repairs and refurbishes them.

Another division of Greenbrier owns and leases over 9100 such cars. It also provides management services for over 216,000 railcars.

In addition, Greenbrier, under the name of Gunderson Marine, manufactures ocean-going barges (over 2000 of them), as well as other vessels, such as tugs. It is also trying to promote habitat values on some of its property.

The largest shipbuilding and repair company in the Northwest is Vigor Industrial, which has operations in Portland and around Puget Sound. The Portland operation, at Swan Island, is the largest of its facilities, with fifteen piers on sixty acres (comprising two-thirds of the company's total pier space). At that location, it is the successor to the 1942 Kaiser Shipyards. In recent years, it has built two ferries there, and many ocean-going barges. It also has an active ship-repair business.

## UNIQUE PRODUCTS

While hand-held chainsaws were not invented in Oregon, the improvements that led to their widespread commercialization were. A design invented by Joseph B. Cox of Portland used alternating C-shaped teeth, thus making it unnecessary to constantly file the saw's blades.

Founded in 1947, Cox's Oregon Saw Chain firm grew into what became Omark Industries. In the 1970s and 80s, improvements were made to reduce kickbacks and improve safety through the development of guard links. In 1985, the company was acquired by Blount industries, which renamed it the Oregon Cutting System; it became a division, with its factory in Milwaukie, Oregon. Its chainsaws now are finding many applications outside the timber industry.

The needs of the Oregon timber industry led to the development of two other firms—each manufacturing equipment for picking up and transporting piles of lumber. One was Hyster (established in 1929), a company that developed the fork-lift truck. The other was Gerlinger (established in 1917), which developed straddle carriers for moving piles of lumber. In due course, both also developed related lines of equipment and were acquired by larger firms.

The Tucker Corporation of Medford produces various vehicles for crossing snowy terrain, including the *Sno-Cat*. Tucker has been in business since 1938, and sells all over the world. Sir Vivian Fuchs used a Sno-Cat in 1958 to cross the Antarctic land mass. In Alaska, they are used in the winter to inspect the oil pipeline and make repairs.

Morrow, a company based in Salem, rents various types of tower cranes and hoist equipment for use in constructing high-rise buildings, as well as gantry cranes for loading/unloading cargo at ports. It has over 750 varied sorts in stock, and has branch offices in twenty-six cities and seven overseas locations.

The Allied Systems Company in Sherwood has been in business for eighty years, producing various vehicles for lifting and transporting heavy materials. It began with vehicles—such as log skidders and the "scoopmobile"— to deliver concrete, and to assist with jobs in the lumber industry. It is now producing marine cranes (winches mounted on bulldozers) and the "long reach" crane attachments for forklifts. Frequently it has produced equipment to meet the needs of the US Navy and Coast Guard. It sells all over the world.

Sno-Cat (Tucker Co. in Medford)

Warn Industries of Clackamas County has been making winches, hoists, and other equipment (in fact, over 600 products) to enhance the performance of vehicles in challenging situations. It has been doing this for many years, and sells around the world.

Entek manufactures microporous membranes used as separators in batteries for trucks and automobiles, as well as in lithium batteries. The polyethylene separators are sold under the **RhinoHide** brand name and are estimated to **have forty percent of the world market**. Founded in 1983, they are located in Lebanon.

Western Shelter Systems in Eugene makes shelters and field gear for crews fighting forest fires; it also sells to the military and to medical teams.

## ATTRACTING ATTENTION

Oregon does well in providing Call Centers for firms because of its location in the Pacific Time Zone and the fact that its workers do not have accented speech (but instead use "general American" speech). Centers are located in many cities in the western part of the state, and a few are located in eastern Oregon. Xerox has two in Portland. Over 12,000 workers are employed in these Call Centers.

The **Umpqua Bank** calls itself the "World's Greatest Bank." It is the largest bank based in Oregon and has been growing rapidly. It has a flat administrative hierarchy in each bank office, and emphasizes good customer relationships. In 2009, it dubbed itself "eco-friendly," and is **ranked highly on *Fortune's* list of the best places to work**. It started in Canyonville in 1953 and has been acquiring other banks. It is now moving into adjoining states.

**Lithia Motors** runs ninety-one automotive dealerships in thirteen western states. In a recent year, it was **on a national list as the fourth most admired firm in its industry**. It sells a wide variety of brands, including German and Japanese brands. Headquartered in Medford, it claims to have a simpler, more straightforward way of dealing with customers. With acquisitions, it has now been listed as a *Fortune 500* company.

HemCon of Portland produces a bandage for the military that is more effective in controlling severe battlefield hemorrhages. Proven to be safe, it has saved hundreds of lives in the recent Middle Eastern wars. It was developed in connection with St. Vincent's Hospital. OHSU has developed a competing product that it claims is even more effective, which is produced by Medix in Lebanon. It is called TraumaStat.

## HIGH-TECH INDUSTRIES (INCLUDING THE "SILICON FOREST" AND INTEL)

The environs of Portland have probably one of the largest concentrations of computer chip fabricating plants in the US. And Portland itself has the second-largest technology output in the country (after Silicon Valley).

Indeed, Oregon is a world center not only for fabricating computer chips, but also for servicing the needs of the computer industry. The economic policy advisor for the governor has gone so far as to claim that "Oregon is **the domi-**

**nant high-tech manufacturing center in the world**." (Vince Porter, the *Oregonian*, 8-27-14).

Oregon's high-tech industry has now eclipsed the timber industry as the state's leading industry (compared to the timber industry at its 1970s height, and looking at percentages of total wages paid in the state). Oregon's high-tech industry now pays twelve percent of all wages in the state.

Depending on one's definition, there are as many as 6100 firms in this manufacturing category. There are at least two dozen firms producing computer chips and related software; these are colloquially known as "Silicon Forest."

Most observers feel that Tektronix helped spark evolution of the industry in Oregon in the 1960s, that Mentor Graphics did in the 1970s, and Intel did in the 1980s. Some regard Howard Vollum, the founder of Tektronix, as the father of the electronics industry in Oregon. Over time, Tektronix spun off a series of electronics firms that later became quite successful: Planar Systems, Tri Quint Semiconductor, Mentor Graphics, and InFocus. As many as forty-eight firms are thought to have been created by former Tektronix employees.

Intel Plant in Hillsboro

Local networking played a major role in the evolution of the Oregon computer industry, as did careful growth at the start. (This is true also of the state's wine and craft-beer industries.)

Those firms that disclose their data have almost $6 billion in revenue. Most have grown even through the most recent recession. The largest, Intel, is not included in these figures, since though it has plants here, its headquarters are elsewhere (taking in $50 billion dollars at all its plants).

There are now nearly 61,000 people employed by Silicon Forest companies. Intel also employs over 18,600 in Oregon, bringing the local tech-worker total to almost 80,000. Counting the 25,000 software workers, there are now

105,000 in the state working in high tech jobs. These jobs typically pay wages that are double the overall state average.

As of this writing, **the largest computer chip production facility in the world** in is at Intel in Hillsboro. This is Intel's largest installation (though the company does have plants in other states and countries). It has a cluster of seven plants in Hillsboro.

Intel was attracted to Oregon by various things:
- state tax breaks (exempting equipment and out-of-state sales, etc.)
- abundant pure water
- inexpensive power
- a stable and well-educated work force
- low housing prices for workers (compared to California)
- low operating costs
- plentiful factory sites

Intel also has a core of talented engineers in Oregon; they developed the Pentium processor there. Hillsboro is the home to Intel's most advanced research and manufacturing facility; each new generation of micro-processors is made there first. The company's **Oregon engineers develop more patents there than anywhere else in its system**, including California. The state also nurtures the most start-ups—as many as forty over the years.

In 2013, Intel completed construction of a new $3 billion D1X research facility in Oregon. It will soon start construction of another fab plant to produce 450 mm wafers.

While Intel is the biggest employer in Oregon, it is also the biggest polluter—though its emissions per employee are not large, and its overall emissions rate has been falling. In 2013-2014, it was criticized by a neighborhood group for not reporting its fluoride emissions; however, it is now reporting and monitoring them.

With a soft worldwide economy and a shift from desktop computers to tablets and cell phones, some think market declines may be in the offing for Intel. Intel is beginning to reduce its staff slightly through offering early retirements. The impact on Oregon remains to be seen.

What is known for certain is that 2014 was the best year ever for sales of computer chips—and two-thirds of Intel's revenue came from selling chips for computers and tablets. Supplying data centers is now a big share of Intel's business as well. The company has also initiated partnerships with Chinese firms to break into the vast Chinese market. Other local chipmakers—e.g., Mentor, FEI, Lattice, Triquint, and Radisys—are also having their best years ever.

## THE REST OF SILICON FOREST

Various other firms offer a variety of computer-related products and services:
- some provide a foundry (TriQuint Semiconductor/Qorvo)
- some design chips (Mentor Graphics, RadiSys, Syniosys, Cipher)
- some manufacture chips (On Semiconductor, Oracle, Lattice Semicoductor, QPL, Lam, Siltronic, Jireh)
- some assemble circuit boards (Merix-Viasystems)
- some test chips (Cascade Microtech, Electro Scientific Industries, Tektronix)
- some recover data after a computer disaster (Symantec)

TriQuint had been the largest of these, but has now merged with an out-of-state firm to form Qorvo, making chips for handsets and networking equipment—the merger put them on the S&P 500 list. Microsoft also has an outpost in Oregon—an engineering office in Wilsonville, acquired when it purchased Perceptive Pixel's operations. And in late 2015, the old Hynix chip-fabricating plant in Eugene was acquired by Avago.

Over 1500 firms in Oregon now design software. The state hosts **the third largest concentration of software designers**—with firms such as Tripwire,

Corillian, Digimark, IBM, Coaxis/Viewpoint, Urban Airship, Jama Software, Opal Labs, Elemental Techologies, and Act-On. The majority of them are in the Portland area, but some are also near Eugene.

Many firms of this nature are moving from the suburbs into downtown Portland to better attract the kind of staff they seek. There seems to be a trend toward California software firms acquiring startup firms in Oregon to obtain their engineering staffs. In many cases, their offices in Oregon are left intact. While acquisition curtails managers' freedom of action, it brings stability to startup firms here and exposes them to larger markets. Many have continued to grow.

The person who designed the Linux system of open-source software, Linus Torvalds, now operates out of Oregon (in Dunthorpe), where he runs the Open Source Development Labs.

### OTHER HIGH-TECH INDUSTRIES

The **Spectra Physics Scanning System** (founded in 1974) is a firm in Eugene that **pioneered the development of barcode scanning devices**. Part of a combine based in Sweden, it sells the most fixed scanners in the world.

FLIR is a fast-growing firm which produces thermal-imaging products for commercial and military use—such as for sensors, cameras, binoculars, and weapons sights. It recently won contracts from the Army and Navy to provide systems for use on helicopters. Worldwide, it employs 3000 people. It has been thriving in recent years, with sales of $1.4 billion.

Another producer of night vision systems is Max-Viz, based in southwest Portland.

Spectron IR in Ashland produces thermal-imaging equipment for medical purposes.

Planar, begun in 1983 as a spin-off from Tektronix, manufactures display screens, monitors, and projectors, and is listed on NASDAQ; it is now growing quickly.

InFocus is a pioneer in making digital projectors and displays for use in business meetings, classrooms, and for home use; most powerpoint presentations use this equipment. It has set the industry standard for large-format, digital displays, though it is facing competition in a changing business environment.

FEI provides the most electron microscopes for nanoscale research in the world market. These are used by researchers in universities and institutes in the fields of electronics and biology, as well as in mining and in oil and gas exploration. Recently it has been enjoying record sales.

Hewlett-Packard started its inkjet printer operation in Corvallis, where its engineers invented their type of inkjet printer. At one time the Corvallis operation was the most profitable of the company's divisions—employing as many as 10,000 people. With the decline of inkjet printer technology, that division has shrunk appreciably.

Epson too has a local inkjet manufacturing facility, in Hillsboro, but with this declining market, it is downsizing and shifting production to Asia. About 1000 people work there now. Xerox has a plant in Wilsonville that produces color-inkjet cartridges, but it is also contemplating layoffs.

Consumer Cellular is a firm, begun in 1995, which offers mobile- phone services for seniors especially. It sells primarily through relationships with AARP and Sears. *Consumer Reports* gives it top ratings as the best choice for seniors. It also offers full-featured smart phones. It has annual revenues of $185 million.

Founded in 1996 and privately held, Integra Telecom is an integrated-telecommunications carrier providing services to businesses in eleven western states. It has an extensive fiber-optic network offering local, long-distance, and broadband services. It has revenues of over $680 million.

Three fiber-optic cable companies have their West Coast landing points in Hillsboro: Southern Cross Cable, VSNL Transpacific, and C2C. Microsoft is in the process of constructing a similar trans-Pacific line from Hillsboro.

Rentrak in Portland uses modern digital analytics to provide precise measurement of the numbers of people viewing movies, broadcast and cable TV programs, and advertisements. It is growing rapidly.

SureID in Portland provides a worldwide service to agencies needing to authenticate workers who seek access to highly secure facilities. It uses biometrics to handle access and reporting. It was originally called Eid Passport.

Elemental encodes media programs and games for online streaming, employing over 200 people. Wacom, which does digital graphics, has moved into Portland's Pearl district. Portland is also attracting a concentration of firms specializing in marketing services for businesses. Firms doing this, such as Lytics and Opal Labs, are growing rapidly.

Portland is now recognized as a place that hosts **an unusual concentration of technology companies that specialize in helping firms meet regulatory compliance requirements** in how they store their records. Some characterize Portland as "the compliance town." Relevant firms include Smarsh, Exterro, Compli, Zaproved, Tripwire, and NAVEX Global.

Rodgers Instruments in Hillsboro manufactures electronic organs for the Roland Company. Rodgers was founded by employees of the Tektronix company who saw the potential for using various transistor and electronic devices to run organs. In due course, they also developed adaptations to assist classical pipe organs. The company was founded in 1958.

Genentech is a California biotech firm begun in 1976; in 2009 it was acquired by Roche pharmaceuticals. That same year it built a plant in Hillsboro to put its products in vials for delivery to doctors; the facility also warehouses its products. Hundreds of workers are employed there.

Micro Power in Beaverton produces lithium-polymer batteries for medical and other devices. It provides portable power sources for handheld devices, such as for computing and medical purposes, and also produces battery packs and thin batteries for both commerce and the military. Founded in 1985, it was recently sold.

Pac Star is a Portland-based firm that has designed military software that provides a single point of access for complex communication systems in the field. It also produces hardware in the form of various kits that implement its software. It sells mainly to the US military and partners with major defense contractors. It is particularly helpful to troops working in rugged terrain with few, if any, cell towers. It originated its special approach in 2008.

Other Oregon high-tech firms design computer software for the military and intelligence community (including the CIA): Tyfone (authentication), SignaCert, and iMove.

Various data centers are being constructed in the Northwest, particularly in Oregon. Oregon now has **one of the largest clusters of these data centers**; they have been drawn here by cheap power, cooling water, and tax breaks. Data centers are operating in Boardman (Amazon and Rackspace); The Dalles (Google); Hillsboro (Adobe Systems, Intel, VIA West, Fortune Data Centers, Digital Realty Trust/Net App, and Telx); Prineville (Apple and Facebook (the latter is Oregon's largest data center)); and Umatilla (Amazon). Puppet Labs in Portland helps manage many of these.

Experts think many more data centers are coming.

It should be added, however, that these centers are not without their drawbacks: they occupy and consume lots of space and power, while providing only limited employment. Many worry that they may want their tax breaks extended indefinitely.

## ENVIRONMENTAL INDUSTRIES

In 2007 German-owned Solar World opened **America's largest plant producing solar-photovoltaic panels**, in Hillsboro. It produces wafers and assembles all the components of panels. It is betting that its design will prove to be the best, and that the US market for solar panels will continue to grow. Its establishment was heavily subsidized by state and local tax credits.

However, this company is facing strong competition from even more heavily subsidized Chinese solar panels, and has filed a trade complaint. It won that complaint, and US duties have been applied at rates between twenty-four and thirty-six percent. While the Solar World decision has been upheld by the US International Trade Commission, China won an appeal to the World Trade Organization (WTO). The US is expected to appeal that ruling.

While the trade dispute raged, Solar World shrunk its work force. But when the market for its panels revived in 2014, it hired another 200 workers. Use of solar roofing has exploded: it is being used on over one million US homes. Installed capacity has jumped ninety times since 2003.

China now faces overcapacity in its solar panel plants. The Chinese industry's future is uncertain because of the costs of its product and its design. Its principal company is facing collapse and has filed for bankruptcy. Experiences with that company's roofing in California have also raised doubts about the reliability of their products.

Sanyo Solar of Oregon has opened a plant in Salem to produce wafers for solar-electric panels, with a design it claims is more efficient than that of its competitors. It is supposed to be particularly effective in cloudy weather. While the wafers for this purpose are grown and sliced at a 130,000-square-foot plant in Salem, the panels are assembled in Japan. Though these panels cost fifteen percent more to make, they are supposed to be twenty-five percent more effective. This plant received subsidies from both the state and the city.

Grape Solar in Eugene assembles panels from foreign components; it opposed Solar World's quest for tariffs on Chinese solar panels, asserting that the tariffs are slowing growth in the market.

Solo Power produces 2000-meter rolls of photovoltaic roofing (without individual silicon wafers). This roofing is designed to go on top of warehouses and "big box" stores—on roofs that will not support heavier panels. The firm claims that this solar roofing will produce power at competitive rates. Founded in 2006 in California, it relocated to north Portland in 2012, and was re-organized in 2013, with new financing.

PV Powered—based in in Bend, Oregon—has developed software to improve connections to the grid of home, solar-power installations. It does this by facilitating the widest range of voltages and temperatures, as well as through the use of inverters. It recently merged with another firm, Advanced Energy.

Danish-owned Vestas (the world's largest manufacture of wind turbines) now maintains its American office in Portland—its only marketing and service center in the United States.

Zea Chem, based in Boardman, produces cellulosic ethanol from woody biomass and wheat straw. It has a hundred regular employees.

SeQuential Pacific Biodiesel, based in Salem, has eighty employees who convert used cooking oil into biodiesel.

Brammo, based in Talent, manufactures electric vehicles; it is expanding its plant to nearly 100,000 square feet.

United Streetcar, owned by Oregon Iron Works and based in Clackamas County, has been the nation's only producer of streetcars. It has suspended production, though.

The United Bicycle Institute, in Ashland, is the **largest national trainer of certified bicycle mechanics**, and the only one anywhere that teaches the techniques of building bicycle frames. In business since 1981, it has trained over 8000 students.

Collins Pine has had its headquarters in Portland for over half a century, operating both in Oregon and in northern California. It is noted for the depth of its commitment to environmentally responsible operations. It was the first timber firm to commit to the rules of the Forest Stewardship Council, as well as the Natural Step.

# CHAPTER 14

# ARTS, CULTURE, AND ENTERTAINMENT

## ARTS AND CULTURE

The Oregon Symphony in Portland is **the oldest orchestra west of the Mississippi**, having completed 115 seasons as of this writing. It is one of the larger orchestras in the nation, employing 76 professional musicians.

The Symphony gives eighty concerts a year, and recently gave a much-heralded concert in New York City. The *New Yorker* called it "pretty extraordinary," and "the most remarkable concert of the regular season." The *New York Times* referred to the orchestra as a "highly polished instrument."

In terms of arts and culture, it is said that musicians and artists in Portland now aspire to be world-class, in contrast to feeling that "mediocrity was good enough for us 25 years ago," as Marty Hughley put it in the *Oregonian*.

The first youth orchestra in America—today known as the Portland Youth Philharmonic—was started in Portland in 1923 by the music teacher Mary Dodge. She came from Burns, where she had begun a similar orchestra known as the "Sagebrush Symphony." The ensemble has toured internationally, made recordings, and performed with the New York Philharmonic, ultimately winning a series of ASCAP awards.

The **Portland Baroque Orchestra** is now thought to be "**within the ranks of the best period-instrument orchestras in North America** and Europe" (as Peter Tear, a New York-based producer, recently put it).

**The Oregon Shakespeare Festival** (in Ashland) is the oldest of this sort in the nation, having operated continuously since it was founded in 1935. It is also **one of the largest professional, regional theaters**, with a staff of 575. In 1983 and 2013, it won regional Tony Awards, as well as being designated as the 2013 "Theatre of the Year" by the National Theatre Conference. It attracts large and faithful audiences, as well as actors and theater artisans from around the world.

Critics have described **Portland Center Stage** as **on a par with the best regional theaters**. The rest of the live theater scene in Portland is thriving, with as many as 125 companies. One observer now sees "Portland **as a player on the national theater scene**."

Portland's Art Museum is the oldest in the Pacific Northwest, having been created in 1892. It has a strong collection of native objects.

Oregon libraries attract **the second-largest clientele in the country, and Portland has the highest per capita use of its library**.

Oregon has more fine museums (relative to its size) than many states. It has twenty of varied sorts: for history, natural history, culture, art, and for things such as cars and airplanes. These are museums having professional polish, curators, and decent collections. They are in many parts of the state: Portland has three; Eugene and Salem each have two; and Ashland, Astoria, Baker City, Bend, The Dalles, Dayville, Eugene, Hood River, McMinnville, Newport, Pendleton, Prineville, Reedsport, and the Tillamook State Forest each have one. In addition, most county seats have local history museums, which vary in quality. The Lane County history museum is probably one of the best.

The annual **Oregon Bach Festival**, based in Eugene, began in 1969 and attracts attendees from all over the world. Students particularly like its classes in conducting. One year, the festival was invited to perform at the Hollywood Bowl. It has made over a dozen recordings. The *New York Times* music critic has called this festival "**the best of its kind in the country**."

The Britt Festival at Jacksonville has been attracting world-class artists for over fifty years. It has been going longer than any almost any comparable festival in the Northwest. It operates for four months each summer, and features music of varied sorts.

Classical musicians from all over the world attend the annual Ernest Bloch Music Festival every summer in Newport and nearby spots; Bloch was a classical composer who lived in that area for a time. The Oregon Coast Music Festival in Coos Bay attracts audiences with similar interests.

Portland hosts a variety of specialized classical groups of distinction; the chamber-music scene is particularly distinguished. 45th Parallel (a nonprofit organization and chamber music group) gets kudos especially for its eclectic programs.

Portland also has a "**tradition of great choral singing**," with high standards. The Oregon Repertory Singers is particularly acclaimed. A group of ninety men and women, it has won first prizes in European competitions and has appeared all over the world. In an American competition for amateur choirs, it gained **the highest score for artistry**. It has been called "one of the finest choral ensembles in America," making dozens of recordings, and collaborating with the Oregon Symphony.

The Portland Symphonic Choir also performs with the Oregon Symphony and tours the world. It has a number of recordings to its credit.

Other distinguished groups in Portland are the:
- Bach Cantata Choir
- Cantores Eccelesia
- Cappella Romana
- Choral Arts Ensemble
- Portland Symphonic Choir
- Portland Vocal Consort

**The largest Christmas choral festival in the world** is held each Christmas in Portland at The Grotto on N.E. Skidmore. In the Christmas season, as many as five groups perform nightly in the Chapel of Mary there.

Oregon has a disproportionately active interest in tracker type (i.e., mechanical) pipe organs, with over two dozen of them in churches in the state. Eight of these were built in the nineteenth century, and fifteen in the twentieth. One dates back to the eighteenth century. In 2014, the *New Yorker* described tracker organs "as one of humanity's grander creations and also one of its more durable technologies." New York City no longer has even one of these.

One of the most spectacular twentieth century pipe organs is the Rosales organ in Portland's Trinity Episcopal Cathedral, which was built in 1987 at a cost of over one million dollars. It has been described as **one of the finest organs anywhere**, and as a "landmark organ of the twentieth century." It has 87 ranks and 4194 pipes.

Another fine new Portland organ is in the First Presbyterian Church, which has a Jaeckel pipe organ, with 69 ranks and 3515 pipes. It was installed in 2000. In 1984, a medieval-style organ was built by Frank Bosman in the Corpus Christi church in the same city; it requires two people to play it.

Oregon also hosts a greater number of builders of pipe organs than one might expect—thirteen over the years. One of these builds electronic organs, and the rest build tracker organs. Richard Bond in Portland and David Petty in Eugene are currently active. John Brombaugh preceded Petty in his Eugene shop, and was widely admired for having built sixty-six pipe organs in twenty-three states. In addition to operating in Portland and Eugene, these builders have operated in Salem, Grants Pass, and Aurora. The electronic firm, Rodgers, operates now out of Hillsboro.

Portland is one of the few cities to host a gathering of pipe organists playing pieces by Johann Sebastian Bach for an afternoon. This concert is called the "Bach-a-Thon" and has been going on annually for a few decades.

Oregon also has an active community of luthiers (makers of stringed instruments). Currently there are seven local luthiers who make violins. Some, such as Jonathan Franke, also make award-winning cellos and violas. Four are in the Eugene area, one is in Portland, and two are in southern Oregon (in Ashland and Phoenix). A former violin maker who lives in Salem—Henry Strobel—now writes books on the art of violin making. Glenn Hill in Phoenix makes

*Arts, Culture, and Entertainment*

Celtic harps and lyres—in fact, he has made almost 500 of them. And Andrew Mowry in Bend makes mandolins.

### POPULAR ENTERTAINMENT

**Oregon Public Broadcasting** (OPB, based in Portland) won a Peabody Award in 2009 and is a major producer for national-public broadcasting of such acclaimed programs as *Rick Steves' Europe*, *Art Wolfe*, *History Detectives*, *Foreign Exchange*, *Barbecue America*, and *Create*. In 2014, OPB won an Emmy Award for excellence in broadcasting. It provides **the most used, and supported, set of services for public broadcasting in the country**.

In 2007 and 2011, **the Portland Rose Festival** was named "**best in the world**" by the International Festivals and Events Association. There are few festivals like it. Its Grand Floral Parade, a tradition begun in 1907, is the second-largest all-floral parade in the US. A number of other parades are held in association with the festival (for instance, the Starlight and Junior Parades), as are the dragon boat races. The festival's associated Royal Rosarians help promote the festival and Oregon.

The Oregon Festival of American Music celebrates music of the Great American Songbook, including jazz and the musical theater, with events running throughout the summer in Eugene. It is one of the few festivals celebrating the popular music of the 1920s-40s.

In 2013, the *New York Times* characterized Portland as "**one of the most exciting music scenes in America**." Portland has dozens of karaoke bars that have caused the city to be called the capital of karaoke in the US.

The band Pink Martini, based in Portland, has a distinctive quality and is invited to perform all over the world, having appeared with fifty established orchestras. It has also been on NPR and the BBC. Twice it has played to sold-out events at Carnegie Hall. The *Washington Post* said it plays "rich, hugely approachable music"—which has been featured in a number of well-received recordings.

Portland's Waterfront Blues Festival is **the largest blues festival west of the Mississippi** (and the second largest in the nation). The jazz festival held each summer in Portland's Cathedral Park (under the St. John's bridge) is the longest-running free-to-the-public jazz festival west of the Mississippi River. Mount Angel's Octoberfest is a bit more modest—merely claiming to be the biggest ethnic-music festival in the Pacific Northwest. But others are less restrained, describing it as **the biggest Octoberfest outside of Bavaria**.

The **Sleater-Kinney band** (based in Portland and originally from Olympia) was called the "**greatest rock band in America**" by *New Yorker* in 2015. Its various albums have been widely acclaimed. One reviewer exclaimed that "they are out here embarrassing every rock band on the planet."

Another Portland band, the Decemberists, have also been hailed as distinguished, and have released seven albums.

The Kingsmen, based in Oregon, had a number of national hits in the mid-1960s—including "Louie Louie" and "Jolly Green Giant." The former has been called one of **the most popular rock and roll songs of all time**. Paul Revere & the Raiders, also based in Oregon, attracted national attention in the mid-1960s, with recordings and hits in the Top 40.

A group of high school students from Portland won a national competition at New York's Lincoln Center in 2015. Playing from memory, and under the leadership of acclaimed trumpeter Thara Memory, they performed one of Duke Ellington's most difficult pieces. They are known as the American Music Program of Portland.

Portland has also been described as a mecca for comic artists and publishers. Some claim the community of cartoonists and graphic artists here is **the largest outside of New York City**. It is clearly the West Coast capital of that industry.

There are now at least seven innovative comic publishers here, including Dark Horse Comics, Periscope Studio, and Oni Press. There are more coming all the time; Heavy Metal, for instance.

Oregon: A State That Stands Out

### FOOD AND DRINK

Oregon has **the largest number of craft breweries per capita**, and the third greatest total number of them (179). Over twenty percent of the beer drunk by Oregon residents is from craft breweries—the highest share in the nation.

With eighty-five breweries, the Portland area not only has **the most craft breweries of any city in the US**—it has the most craft breweries of any city in the world. Its craft breweries won nine gold medals at the World Beer Cup in 2014—an event put on by the Craft Brewers Conference. In 2015, its craft beers won seven gold medals in Denver at the Great America Beer Festival, the most of any state on a per capita basis. Bend also has a high number of microbreweries, especially when viewed on a per capita basis—twenty-six. The Pelican Brewery and Pub in Pacific City is probably the only brewery right on the ocean.

Craft distilleries are also thriving in Oregon, with forty-eight of them making drinks such as fruit-based vodka. And shops in Portland, such as Pix Patisserie, have won international awards for their wines and sherries.

Portland has a **world-renowned food cart scene**, made up of over 400 food carts. These are regularly reviewed by food critics in area media. They often feature folk food from various countries. Moreover, the regulatory climate makes it easier for small entrepreneurs to get started in this business, instigating a micro-economy. The carts in turn invigorate the street scene.

Food Cart in Portland

Some of Portland's **indoor restaurants** have distinguished, long-term reputations, **drawing favorable reviews nationally**. They include Bluehour, Castagnas, The Heathman Restaurant, Higgins, Noble Rot, and Paley's Place. Le Pigeon, the Beast, and Pok Pok were on a 2014 list of the 101 Best Restaurants in America (curated by the *Daily Meal*); Pok Pok was given two stars (i.e., very good) by the *New York Times* food critic.

Five other Oregon restaurants have been listed as among the 100 Best Restaurants in America: Bend's Ariana restaurant, the Painted Lady and the Joel

Palmer House in the upper Willamette valley, and Portland's Natural Selection and Roe.

Portland's **Gabriel Rucker has twice won the James Beard Award (which some consider the "Oscars of Food")**, as well as once having been named the best young chef in the country. Nine other chefs working in Portland have also received this award—including Greg Higgins, Vitaly Paley, and Philippe Boulot. And the *New York Times* has called Naomi Pomeroy, of the Beast, "a cooking-world star."

Portland has been called "**the great new American food city**" (*Oregonian*, May 12, 2013; see also *The Mighty Gastropolis: Portland*, by Karen Brooks, Chronicle Books, 2013). Portland and the surrounding area are "well known in the US as a food mecca and for pushing culinary trends," observes an executive for California's Diamond Foods.

The *New York Times* has written that Portland "has **one of the most distinctive tea scenes in the country**." Various specialty firms that blend teas have originated in that city or elsewhere in the state—Stash, Tazo, Oregon Chai, Yogi, and Steven Smith's teas are examples. Unusual tea houses have set up business in Portland.

Some concluding food-based trivia:

Portland's Franz Family Bakery invented the modern hamburger bun.

The city's Voodoo Donuts has attracted national media attention; they are in *Guinness World Records* for the "biggest box of donuts."

Lauretta Jean's Pie Shop—on SE Division in Portland—is on a list of the country's ten best pie shops.

## MISCELLANEOUS

In 2002 Katie Harmon of Oregon won the Miss America contest.

In 2015, the AARP listed Portland as **among the ten most livable (and healthiest) cities**, as well as the easiest in which to get around, and the easiest in which to make friends. It was also the first city in the US named to the

Global Network of Age-Friendly Cities and Communities by the World Health Organization.

Nearby Sherwood was recently named as **one of the six most desirable places in the country to live** by *Money* magazine. It was accorded this status by virtue of various things: good schools, affordable homes, good job opportunities, and a robust arts scene. And Bend is one of the ten fastest- growing cities.

Portland has **the nation's largest continuously operating open-air crafts market**: Portland's Saturday Market.

Portland has the **highest number of movie theater seats (evaluated on a per capita basis)**.

Portland has now been found to be among the world's top ten most literary cities (by *Highbrow Magazine*, among others).

The Multnomah County Library is **one of the highest rated in the country**, and one of the busiest (in 2014, it was rated five star by *Library Journal*).

Portland's Zoo has the most successful program in the world for breeding Asiatic elephants—although elephants there still have problems with their feet, as a result of being too confined. The zoo also has programs for saving over fifty endangered and threatened species. The aquarium in Seaside was the first to successfully breed harbor seals in captivity.

In 2011, Portland's Lone Fir cemetery was recognized as one of the top ten cemeteries in the country by the *National Geographic Travelers* magazine.

The longest-running sheepdog competition west of the Mississippi is held in Scio, Oregon. It has been held annually since 1937.

Portland's Museum of Science and Industry (OMSI), for children, is one of the most distinguished of its type in the US.

Since 2001, a five-day independent film festival has been held in Ashland. Oregon has a growing scene of independent filmmakers. Film festivals are also held in Astoria, Bend, Eugene, and Salem.

The statue of **Portlandia** in Portland is **the largest hammered-copper statue west of the Mississippi**. Nationally, it is second in size only to the Statue of Liberty. In its present location, it is hard to see. In 1998, Portland citizens tried to have it moved to a better location, but could not get approval.

Oregon has a nationally noteworthy number of statues commemorating the history of the West and its settlement. These include:

*The Lewis and Clark Memorial Column* (1908) in Washington Park

*Sacajawea and Jean-Baptiste* (1905), also in that park

*The End of the Trail* (1990), a statue of Lewis and Clark in the roundabout in Seaside

*The Pioneer* (1919), in Eugene on the University of Oregon grounds

*The Pioneer Mother* (1932), also on those grounds

*The Circuit Rider* (1924), in Salem on the capitol grounds

*The Willamette Stone* in the west hills of Portland (the geographical point at which surveys in Oregon began to facilitate settlement)

*Elk* (1900), on Portland's Plaza Blocks

*The Spanish-American War Soldier's Monument* (1906), also on the Plaza Blocks, and

*Theodore Roosevelt, Rough Rider* (1922) on Portland's South Park Blocks

Lewis and Clark Statue in Seaside

A few other monuments in the state are on the National Register: the Astoria Victory Monument (1926; commemorating victory in World War I), and the Portland Firefighter's Park (1928).

Worthy of being on the National Register are the Skidmore Fountain (1888), in Portland's Old Town, and Portland's Shemanski Fountain (1926) on its South Park Blocks. The Shemanski Fountain includes a wonderful small bronze statue: *Rebecca at the Well*. The Skidmore Fountain features a memorable quote by C.E.S. Wood: "Good Citizens Are the Riches of a City."

Portland also has two fountains in parks designed by noted landscape architect Lawrence Halprin: the Lovejoy Fountain Park (1963) and the Keller Fountain Park (1968). Both are designed to suggest streams splashing down rock ledges in Oregon. They exemplify the modern tastes of the mid-twentieth

Oregon: A State That Stands Out

Multnomah Falls

century (featuring austere, rectangular shapes)—though some viewers might prefer a more naturalistic approach. Nonetheless, they have attracted international attention.

The Oregon Historical Society has the most complete historical library in the PNW. At one time, it had the highest per capita membership at 8000. In its prime, it was among the state historical societies with the most varied features: a research library, a collection of historical artifacts, a museum, a journal, an oral-history program, and a book-publishing program.

The world's largest collection of carousel horses is found in a museum in Hood River.

While a graduate student at Reed College in the late 1930s, Italian designer Emelio Pucci organized a ski team there and outfitted them in stylish outfits.

Nationally acclaimed resorts in scenic places in or near Oregon's federal reserves include: the Lodge at Crater Lake National Park, Timberline Lodge in the Mt. Hood National Recreation Area, and the Lodge at the Oregon Caves National Monument. The Lodge at Multnomah Falls is also generally thought to belong on this list, but it does not provide overnight accommodations anymore—only a restaurant. Designed in classic rustic style by A.E. Doyle in 1925, the City of Portland funded it after thwarting efforts to log the area. Its nearby falls are one of the most-visited natural sites in Oregon.

The most acclaimed private scenic resorts are the Stephanie Inn at Cannon Beach; Salishan at Gleneden Beach; the Sun River Lodge, a dozen miles south of Bend; the Tetherow Lodges, in Bend; the Brasada Ranch Lodge east of Bend; the

Five Pines Lodge in Sisters; the Black Butte Ranch west of Sisters—once rated by Conde Nast as among the world's top resorts; and the Tu Tu Tun Lodge in Gold Beach, on the Rogue River—often rated as one of the best small resorts.

In the 2015 AAA travel guide, fifteen hotels in Oregon earned a "Four Diamond" rating.

The travel industry in Oregon generates over $10 billion each year.

WELL-KNOWN PEOPLE WHO HAVE LIVED IN OREGON

Oregon has been home for a number of well-known people:

**Politicians and Activists**: President Herbert Hoover (grew up in Oregon), Governor Tom McCall, Senator Charles McNary (one-time candidate for Vice President), national suffragist leader Abigail Scott Duniway, Indian leader Chief Joseph

**Scientists**: Linus Pauling (winner of two Nobel prizes), Botanist: Thomas J. Howell (Flora of the Northwest)

**Actors and Directors:** Jane Powell, Ginger Rogers, Clark Gable (as a young adult), Kim Novak (in retirement), Sally Struthers, James Gleason, Danny Glover, William Hurt, Walter Brennan (ranch near Joseph), John Wayne (part owner of ranch near Selma), Patrick Duffy, Sam Elliott, Edgar Buchanan, Margaux Hemingway, River Phoenix, Edy Williams, Lindsay Wagner, Jim Belushi (cabin at Eagle Point), James Ivory (director), Gus Van Sant (director), Mel Blanc (voice of animated creatures), Vance Colvig (voice of Disney's Goofy)

Black Butte Ranch

**Food Critics and Chefs:** James Beard ("Dean of American Cookery"), Gabriel Rucker (two-time winner of the James Beard Award)

**Religious Leaders:** Evangelist Billy Sunday (owned a summer place in the Hood River Valley)

**Animators/Cartoonists:** Matt Groening (creator of *The Simpsons*), early-twentieth-century political cartoonist Homer Davenport from Silverton (perhaps best known for his work with Hearst's *San Francisco Examiner*)

**Journalists:** Nicholas Kristoff (*New York Times*), Ann Curry (news television), Richard L. Neuberger (magazine writer, politician)

**Musicians:** Doc Severinsen, Chris Botti, Courtney Love, Nancy King, Johnnie Ray (a dozen gold records), Mason Williams, Ernest Bloch, Jim Pepper, Storm Large, Thomas Lauderdale, Morten Lauridsen (America's greatest living choral composer)

**Authors:** H. L. Davis, Ernest Haycox, Stewart Holbrook, Jean M. Auel, Raymond Carver, Ursula K. Le Guin, John Reed, Ken Kesey, Richard Brautigan, Chuck Palahniuk, Bernard Malamud (wrote here for a dozen years), Barry Lopez (poet), Gary Snyder, (poet), William Stafford (poet, won a National Book Award), Hazel Hall (poet), Alvin Josephy (ranch at Joseph), and Don Berry; Beverly Cleary, Clare Newberry, and Colin Meloy (also of the rock band the Decemberists) are all authors of books for children

**Artists/Photographers:** Richard Diebenkorn, Mark Rothko, C.S. Price, Minor White, Ray Atkeson; Designer of Kinetic Animals: Michael Curry (Scappoose) a production designer specializing in transformational scenery, large-scale puppetry, costuming, and character design

**Athletes/celebrities:** Steve Prefontaine, Roddy Piper (wrestler), Randy Couture (mixed martial arts), Norm Van Brocklin, Dan Fouts, Tonya Harding

Other famous Oregonians (or Oregon institutions) have won Pulitzer Prizes (fourteen) and Congressional Medals of Honor (thirteen). Five Oregonians have been astronauts. Five of the *Oregonian*'s Pulitzers have been won since

1999, but two were won in earlier years (1939 and 1957). The *Medford Mail Tribune* won one in 1934.

## FILMS, TELEVISION PROGRAMS, AND NOVELS SET IN OREGON

Nearly fifty silent films were shot in Oregon, including Buster Keaton's *The General*. Over 250 "talkies" have been filmed here as well—in whole or in part. Among the best known are:

> *Big Timber, Abe Lincoln in Illinois, Rachel and the Stranger, Lost Horizon, Canyon Passage, Bend of the River, Indian Fighter, Ring of Fire, Emperor of the North, Oregon Passage, Shenandoah, Paint Your Wagon, The Way West, The Great Race, Five Easy Pieces, Sometimes a Great Notion, The Great Northfield Minnesota Raid, Lost Horizon, Rooster Cogburn, One Flew Over the Cuckoo's Nest, The Apple Dumpling Gang, National Lampoon's Animal House, The Shining, Personal Best, Hell and High Water, The Adventures of Mark Twain, The Goonies, Stand by Me, Inherit the Wind, Moonwalker, Drugstore Cowboy, Even Cowgirls Get the Blues, Free Willy, Free Willy II, Fire in the Sky, Mr. Holland's Opus, Grizzly Mountain, Foxfire, Harvest of Fear, Fahrenheit 9/11, Are We There Yet?, The River Why, River Wild,* and *What the Bleep Do We Know!?*

In the 1920s, Beaverton even had a film studio producing such silent films as *Flames of Passion* (1923) and *Shackles of Fear* (1924). This studio was called Premium Picture Productions.

Today Oregon has one studio—**Laika**—which produces animated films using the stop-action technique (one recent example is *Coraline*). Laika is located in Hillsboro on Highway 26, and is owned by Phil Knight and run by his son, Travis. Its first two animated films were nominated for Academy Awards. In 2012, it won the top animation award (the "Annie") for *Para-Norman*.

Oregon: A State That Stands Out

Four national TV shows have recently been situated and shot in Portland: *Portlandia* (which won a Peabody Award in 2011), *Grimm*, *Leverage*, and *The Librarians*. Another—*Backstrom*—is supposedly situated there, but is really shot in Vancouver, British Columbia. There is a studio for shooting television shows on route 212, in Oregon's Clackamas County.

Over two dozen **novels** have been set in Oregon. Among them are:

*Fight Club* by Chuck Palahniuk
*Gone, But Not Forgotten* by Phillip Margolin
*The Hawkline Monster* by Richard Brautigan
*Honey in the Horn* by H. L. Davis (won a Pulitzer Prize)
*Lathe of Heaven* by Ursula K. Le Guin
*One Flew Over the Cuckoo's Nest* and *Sometimes a Great Notion*, both
    by Ken Kesey
*Astoria* by Washington Irving
*Oregon Detours* and *Swift Flows the Rivers*, both by Nard Jones
*Ricochet River* by Robin Cody
*Trask* by Don Berry
various crime novels by Chelsea Cain (including *Heartsick*)
various westerns by Zane Grey (including *Rogue River Feud* (1929)
    Grey had a fishing cabin at Winkle Bar on the Rogue
Frank Herbert's celebrated science fiction novel, *Dune*, was inspired
    by a visit to the Oregon Dunes

### SONGS FEATURING OREGON

"Louie Louie" (originally recorded by Richard Berry in 1957) was recorded by the Portland-based Kingsmen in 1963, and reached number two on the Billboard charts; this version was later featured in the film *Animal House*. Soundwaves from the recording are depicted on plastic panels on the new federal building in Portland.

About a dozen popular songs have been written about Portland, including:
"Portland Town to Klamath" (1941) by Woody Guthrie
"Portland Oregon You're My Home" (2010) by Carrie Brownstein
"Light Rail Coyote" (2002) by Sleater-Kinney
"Portland, Oregon" (2004) by Loretta Lynn & Jack White
"On the Bus Mall" (2005) by The Decemberists
"Portland Rain" (2006) by Everclear
Various songs also feature Eugene—including "Eugene, Oregon," by Dolly Parton (2009).

*Arts, Culture, and Entertainment*

# CHAPTER 15

# UNIVERSITIES IN OREGON: STANDING AND ACCOMPLISHMENTS

The faculties of Oregon's public universities rank among the top ten percent of faculties in American colleges and universities earning federal research grants.

### OREGON HEALTH & SCIENCE UNIVERSITY (OHSU)

At the national level, **OHSU is one of the highest-ranking state medical schools**. *U.S. News & World Report* ranked it second for teaching about family medicine and primary care, and fifth about rural care. It assumed its present form as Oregon's mainstream medical school in 1974.

OHSU's Dr. Robert Kohler discovered a way to administer a blood test for diabetes that has since become standard. It was at OHSU's Knight Cancer Institute that the groundbreaking cancer drug, Gleevec, was developed. Also at OHSU, Dr. Albert Starr developed the Starr-Edwards heart valve—now in use all over the world. For this he was awarded the Albert Lasker prize in 2007. OHSU installs more of these devices than anywhere else west of the Mississippi.

### OREGON STATE UNIVERSITY (OSU)

The Carnegie Foundation puts **OSU into the category of top-tier research institutions**. It is a leading research institution in marine science, forestry, climate change, wave energy, public health, and sustainable food production. It is one of only two US institutions to qualify for grants in all of the following categories: land, sea, sun, and space.

OSU recently had a sixty-three percent increase in the fees it receives from licensing new technologies. During the Great Recession of 2008, its grant revenues held steady. Recently it collaborated with the University of Oregon's green chemistry program to procure a $20 million grant from the National Science Foundation to promote sustainable chemistry and to develop materials in a way that would have minimal environmental impact.

Scientists at OSU have steadily found ways to improve the productivity of Oregon's agriculture. They have also made discoveries in the marine environment, adding to scientists' knowledge of black smokers, for instance. The school is also noted for its research on whales and ocean acidification. Its graduates have made technological discoveries, such as microbial fuel cells and computer mouses.

OSU has developed a new electronic device to monitor people's vital signs. And it has also discovered how to remove stem cells from cloned embryos.

John Wager, one of the school's electrical engineers, led the way in the discovery of an oxide-film technology that is now being used in components of Apple's display panels. Moreover, it has learned how to improve the process for turning waste into electricity through the use of compounds made by microwave energy.

Its forest scientists have developed a way to turn low-density wood from young forests into hard, high-density products, such as flooring. OSU also has invented a pressure-sensitive glue that is inexpensive and environmentally safe.

Jane Lubchenco, OSU professor of marine biology, headed the National Oceanic and Atmospheric Administration from 2009-2013. In 1997, she was also the president of the National Association for the Advancement of Science.

## UNIVERSITY OF OREGON (U OF O)

U of O is consistently ranked high among research universities—typically in the top 8 percent. Among its alumni are 2 Nobel Prize winners, 10 Pulitzer Prize winners, 13 Rhodes Scholars, 58 Guggenheim Fellows, and 129 Fulbright Scholars.

U of O's Institute of Molecular Biology has achieved world-class status in the quality of its research and its results.

Its Mathematics Department is highly rated among mathematics departments in the country.

In 2015, its **architecture program** was ranked as **the best in sustainable design** by *Design Intelligence* magazine and the publication *America's Best Architecture and Design Schools.*

The **U of O** has a nationally acknowledged **green chemistry program**; the *New York Times* believes it is **a leader in this movement**. It promotes innovation and new products that are sustainable and reduce the use of risky chemicals.

Chemistry professor Geraldine Richmond was chosen to serve as the president of the American Association for the Advancement of Science in 2014; she is also on the National Science Board.

U of O's Lundquist School of Business is listed as being among the best undergraduate programs in business, according to *U.S. News and World Report* (2013). Lundquist also has the first program in Sports Management, offering bachelor's and master's degrees. It was **the first business school in the country to place a sports-management program in a business school**, and now it is extending this program to include sports products.

U of O's programs in architecture, geography, and education are also highly ranked.

### REED COLLEGE (PORTLAND)

Loren Pope, a former education editor for the *New York Times*, characterizes **Reed as "the most intellectual college in the country."** In 2005, the *Princeton Review* put it "first in the overall Undergraduate Academic Experience." A very high percentage of its graduates go on to earn PhDs. It is second in the number of Rhodes Scholarships its students have been awarded.

## PORTLAND STATE UNIVERSITY (PSU)

PSU is the largest and fastest-growing university in Oregon. In 2012 and 2013, it was listed by *U.S. News & World Report* as one of the top ten "up and coming universities." These are the universities defined by the magazine as making "the most promising and innovative changes in the areas of academics, faculty, student life, campus, or facilities." PSU has been said to be "a college with a conscience" and is ranked as one of the top Green Schools. It puts special emphasis on sustainability.

Among its highly regarded programs are those for Urban and Regional Planning.

It is regarded as having **one of the best engineering programs for undergraduates**.

In a joint initiative with OHSU, it has established **the first program for biomedical informatics**.

Its chemistry professor, David Peyton, is leading the way in developing hybrid drugs that will not be disabled by disease-resistant variants.

Reed College in Portland

## OREGON INSTITUTE OF TECHNOLOGY (WILSONVILLE)

This rather new institution was tied for first place among regional public colleges in the 2015 ratings of *U.S. News & World Report*.

## LEWIS & CLARK COLLEGE

This prestigious school has nationally ranked programs in biology, psychology, and environmental studies. It is **among the top ten colleges studying clean technology**. All its power is from wind power. According to some surveys, it is one of the ten greenest colleges. Its campus has also been ranked as the second most beautiful in the nation, given its location next to the Lloyd Frank estate.

### UNIVERSITY OF PORTLAND

Among universities with masters' programs, the University of Portland has been **among the top producers of Fulbright scholars**, particularly in the 2000s. In fact, in 2012, it was *the* top producer. While this institution grew out of a religiously oriented college, today it has a school of engineering, a business school, and a nursing school.

### WILLAMETTE UNIVERSITY (SALEM)

In 2008, the *Princeton Review* described this institution as "academically rigorous, intimate, and gorgeous." Among its notable graduates are former Oregon senators Mark Hatfield and Bob Packwood.

### PACIFIC UNIVERSITY (FOREST GROVE)

Pacific University is regularly named as one of the top regional post-secondary institutions in the West. Its (low residency) MFA program has been named as one of the top five in the nation. It offers a doctorate in optometry. It has branches in Hillsboro and Eugene.

### LINFIELD COLLEGE (McMINNVILLE)

In 2010, Linfield was among the top producers of Fulbright scholars. That year, the *Princeton Review* described it as **among the top small colleges in the West**.

### GEORGE FOX UNIVERSITY (NEWBERG)

This small Quaker University grew out of an academy founded in 1885 (and once attended by President Herbert Hoover). *Forbes* magazine recently named it as the best Christian college in the nation.

# CHAPTER 16

# ACHIEVEMENT IN SPORTS

## FOOTBALL

**The University of Oregon** (known colloquially as "U of O," or by their mascot, the Ducks) played in the Rose Bowl in 1917, 1920, 1957, 1995, 2010, 2012, and 2015—winning in 1917, 2012, and 2015. It played in the BCS national championship game in 2011, and before then in other BCS bowl games. Altogether, U of O has played in nineteen bowl games since winning the Independence Bowl game in 1989.

In 2014-15, U of O was the PAC 12 champion. In that season, it was ranked second in the nation. And in that year, it won one of the national playoff games decisively (59-20).

Oregon has held the NCAA record for the most consecutive games in which it has thrown for a touchdown (seventy games).

The U of O has sent fifteen skilled quarterbacks to the pro leagues. Among them have been Norm Van Brocklin (who led Philadelphia to win the championship in 1960), Bob Berry, Dan Fouts, Chris Miller, Bill Musgrave, Joey Harrington, and now Marcus Mariota.

In 2014, Mariota, of the U of O, won the Heisman Trophy, as well as many other awards bestowed on top quarterbacks. In that year, he was also the Associated Press Player of the Year. In his debut in the pros, he had the top efficiency rating.

In 2015, as quarterback for the U of O, Vernon Adams, Jr., had the top efficiency rating in passing for a college player—179.1. He also had the most yards gained in every attempt—10.2 yards.

**Oregon State University** (also known by their mascot, the Beavers) has played in three Rose Bowl games, winning one. It has also played in ten other bowl games, winning the majority of them. In 1962, Terry Baker won the Heisman Trophy. In 2014, OSU's quarterback, Sean Mannion, set a PAC 12 record for the number of passes he completed. Mannion has gone on to play professional football.

**Linfield College** won four national titles in the NCAA's Division III, and then Division II, football—in 1982, 1984, 1986, and 2004. It has had fifty-seven consecutive winning seasons—the longest winning streak in football of any college in the country. Its Brett Elliott became a quarterback with the San Diego Chargers.

**Portland State University's** Neil Lomax went to the St. Louis Cardinals as a quarterback in the mid-1980s, and played there for ten years. He has since been inducted into the National Football Hall of Fame.

**Southern Oregon University** won the National Association of Intercollegiate Athletics (NAIA) football championship in 2014.

Nearly eighty players from Oregon colleges later went on to play for professional football teams. Of them, five were eventually inducted into the Football Hall of Fame. These were quarterbacks Norm Van Brocklin and Dan Fouts, tackle Gary Zimmerman, linebacker Dave Wilcox, and cornerback Mel Refro.

Drew Bledsoe, a champion quarterback with the New England Patriots, retired to Bend, Oregon, after a career in which he won a Super Bowl and played in four Pro Bowls. Bledsoe set a number of records, but is not yet eligible for induction into the Football Hall of Fame. Ryan Longwell, who grew up in Bend, was a kicker in the NFL. He played in one Super Bowl, and once kicked a fifty-four-yard field goal. While with the Green Bay Packers, he kicked the most field goals in the team's history.

BASEBALL

A University of Oregon graduate, **Joe Gordon**, played in the professional leagues and was inducted into the Baseball Hall of Fame. He was called the **"finest second baseman in Major League history."** He played for the New York Yankees and the Cleveland Indians.

Bobby Doerr, who late in life lived in Oregon, spent his professional career with the Boston Red Sox—later becoming a coach. Playing as a second baseman, he set several records. He was inducted into the Baseball Hall of Fame in 1986.

Earl Averill, Jr., was also inducted into the Baseball Hall of Fame. A catcher, he played for the University of Oregon, where he was their first All-American. Professionally, he played for five major-league teams.

Dale Murphy of Portland played professionally for the Atlanta Braves and the Philadelphia Phillies, beginning in 1980. He was once his league's Most Valuable Player. Dave Kingman, born in Pendleton, played professionally for eight different teams, and was known for his 442 home runs; he was twice the home-run champion (meaning he had the most in a given year). He was an all-star for three years.

Johnny Pesky of Portland played professionally for a number of teams, but was most closely associated with the Boston Red Sox, where he played shortstop for seven years; he also had a top record as a hitter. Later, he would become a coach, manager, and color commentator.

**Oregon State University**'s baseball team won the national championship in 2006 and 2007, and has reached the college world series five times. It was the PAC 12 champion in 2013.

By 2015, the **University of Oregon** Women's Softball team had won three straight PAC-12 championships. That same year, it achieved a record number of wins.

**Linfield College** has won two NCAA Division III softball championships—one in 2007 and one in 2011.

*Achievement in Sports*

Linfield also won the NCAA Division III baseball championship in 2013, with a 42-8 season.

**George Fox University** won the Division III championship in 2004.

A minor-league baseball team, the **Portland Beavers**, won pennants in 1910 and 1911, again in 1936 and 1985, and continued until they moved away in 2010. Six players who started out with the Beavers, and then played in the major leagues, eventually were inducted into Baseball Hall of Fame. Minor-league, professional baseball returned to the Portland metro area in 2013 when the Yakima team re-located to become the Hillsboro Hops, and proceeded to win the title in that league for two years in a row: 2014 and 2015.

When the Portland Beavers were away in the mid-1970s, an independent and eccentric professional baseball team came to Portland—the Maverick**s**, which had five winning seasons, including the league championship in 1977.

## BASKETBALL

The **University of Oregon** won the NCAA men's basketball championship in 1939, with a 29-5 record. Its team was known as the "Tall Firs."

In 2013, the team went to the NCAA tournament and advanced to the "sweet 16" stage, going as the PAC 12 champion. It went to the NCAA tournament again in 2015. In 2016, that team won the PAC-12 championship, its tournament, and advanced to the "Elite Eight" stage of the NCAA tournament. And its coach, Dana Altman, was named the college coach of the year for men's basketball.

**Oregon State University** has been to the NCAA tournament sixteen times, making it to the "final four" twice. In 2016, its women's team won the PAC 12 women's tournament and reached the final-four stage of the NCAA tournament..

**George Fox University**'s women's basketball team won the Division III championship in 2009, with no losses. Its women's basketball team also played in the Division III title game in 2012, after an undefeated season. And it has more undefeated seasons in 2014-15 and again in 2015-16.

**Oregon Institute of Technology**'s men's basketball team has the longest winning-streak at home. It won the Division II national championship in 2004 and 2008.

The **Portland Trailblazers**—the state's professional team—won the national championship in 1977 and made NBA final appearances in 1990 and 1992. It has qualified for the playoffs in twenty-nine seasons, including a streak of twenty-one appearances from 1983-2003—the second-longest such streak in the NBA.

Various players from Oregon are now playing elsewhere professionally. Kevin Love (from Lake Oswego) plays for Cleveland, Kyle Singler (from Medford) plays for Oklahoma City, and Mike Dunleavy (from the Portland area) plays for Chicago.

## TRACK AND FIELD

In recent years, the **University of Oregon** has won 12 NCAA championships in cross-country and track and field events combined, including in 2014 and 2015. The school's dominance is so pronounced that its home field is now called "Track Town, USA."

When Steve Prefontaine was there, he set 13 NCAA records and won seven NCAA championships. Rudy Chapa won the national cross-country championship in 1977, as well as championships later in the 3000- and 5000-meter events. When Alberto Salazar was on the team, he won the 1979 US cross-country championship. At various times, he set records in winning the New York marathon three times, as well as the Boston marathon.

The University of Oregon's Galen Rupp recently won the NCAA distance records, as well as the gold medal for the 10,000-meter race in the 2012 Olympics, and he keeps winning that event. Ashton Eaton, who trained at the University of Oregon, is the reigning world-record holder in the decathlon event.

*Achievement in Sports*

Mack Robinson, who attended the University of Oregon, won a silver medal as a member of the 1936 US Olympic team; he finished just behind gold medalist Jesse Owens. He was a brother of baseball legend Jackie Robinson.

At the 1960 Summer Olympics, a University of Oregon runner, Otis Davis, won two gold medals, setting a record in the 400-meter event. Both Robinson and Davis were among the many runners from Oregon who won Olympic events. Seven runners from the University of Oregon have been inducted into the National Track and Field Hall of Fame.

**Bill Bowerman** was the first track and field coach for the University of Oregon. He **brought its teams into the top ranks, winning twenty-two NCAA championships, and training thirty-one Olympic medalists and sixty-four All-Americans.** He also trained twelve American record holders. His teams were undefeated in ten seasons. He coached the US team at the 1972 Olympics in Munich. Moreover, he introduced jogging into the United States.

Along with Phil Knight, who had once run for him at the University of Oregon, Bowerman started **Nike**. Bowerman used his wife's waffle iron to form the soles of his first running shoes, and later was involved in the firm's design process. Nike soon **became the largest and most successful marketer of running shoes in the world**.

For thirty years, Nike has sponsored the annual "Hood to Coast Relay," a 200-mile footrace from Mt. Hood to the coast. It claims to be the largest such race in the world, attracting as many as 12,000 participants, and raising money for charity.

The Oregon Track Club (in Eugene) trains contenders for the Olympics. The Nike Oregon Project (in the Portland area) trains athletes for the highest level of track-and-field performance.

The University of Portland often puts forth one of the NCAA's Division I top cross-country teams, with one of the longest conference divisional championship streaks.

## MISCELLANEOUS

The Athletic program at **the University of Oregon draws the most financial support of any NCAA Division I program**: in the 2013-14 season, it collected $196 million.

Sports fans seem to like loud stadiums, and the University of Oregon's Autzen Stadium is reputed to be one of the loudest, measuring as high as 127 decibels at one football game. Some think loudness arises out of the design of the stadium—either its steep stands or the overhang of its press box. Others think the fans there are just noisy and have a lot to cheer about.

Danny Ainge, born in Eugene, played professionally in both baseball (with the Toronto Blue Jays) and basketball (with various teams, including the Boston Celtics and the Portland Trail Blazers). At the high school level, Ainge was the only athlete ever to be named an All-American in football, basketball, and baseball.

Frank Troeh, who spent much of his adult life in Portland, was a championship trap shooter. He won gold and silver medals in that event in the 1920 Summer Olympics in Antwerp.

## GOLF

Various people from Oregon have been successful as professional golfers.

For instance, Bob Gilder from Corvallis turned professional in 1973 and had twenty-four wins in his professional career. He was also a member of the 1983 winning Ryder Cup team.

Peter Jacobsen, from Portland, turned professional in 1976 and had seven wins on PGA tours, and two more wins as a senior golfer. He played as a member of the Ryder Cup team twice: in 1985 and 1995.

Brian Henninger, who lives in Wilsonville, turned professional in 1987 and won two PGA tours as well as three tournaments in nationwide tours.

John Fought of Portland turned professional in 1977 and had two wins on PGA tours. When he was an amateur, he was a member of a winning Walker Cup team.

*Achievement in Sports*

Among amateurs from Oregon, a number are remembered. Dick Yost was a member of the Walker Cup team in 1955, along with Bruce Cudd. Cudd also won the Western Amateur championship the year before.

Don Moe won the Western Amateur twice, in 1929 and 1931. He too was a member of the Walker Cup teams in 1930 and 1932. Before then, in 1924, Oscar Willing too was a member of Walker Cup team.

Mary Budke of Dayton won the USGA Women's Amateur Golf Championship in 1972 and the PNGA Women's Amateur Golf Championship in 1976. She was also a member of the Curtis Cup Team in 1974.

Grace DeMoss of Corvallis was also a member of the US Curtis Cup team twice, in 1952 and 1954. In 1949, she had won the Canadian Women's Amateur Championship.

In new version of golf called "speed golf," a Lake Oswego high-schooler, Mark Stockamp, won an international tournament in 2012. "Speed golf" puts a premium on speed as well as a high score.

## HOCKEY

Portland's professional hockey team, the Winterhawks, won the 2012-13 league championship of the Western Hockey league. It had previously won this championship in 1997-98 and 1979-80.

## RODEO RIDING

Larry Mahan, of Brooks, won all sorts of recognition as a rodeo rider. He was the All-Around Rodeo champion for five years in a row: from 1966 to 1970, and then again in 1973. He was inducted into the National Rodeo Hall of Fame in 1966, and into the Pro Rodeo Hall of Fame in 1979.

Before him, in 1934, Leonard Ward, from Talent, was the first American to win a Triple Crown in world championships: in bronco riding, steer decorating, bull riding, and bareback riding.

## SOCCER

In the 1970s and early 1980s, Portland had a professional soccer team that enjoyed almost instant success, getting quickly to the Soccer Bowl. Portland then became known as "Soccer City USA." It made it to the playoffs in 1975, 1978, and 1981. Subsequently that team declined and left. Major soccer returned to Portland in 2009. All the professional men's soccer teams that have been in Portland have been called **"the Timbers." In 2015 that team won the national Major League Soccer championship.**

**In 2013, the women's professional soccer team in Portland, the Thorns, won the National Women's Soccer League title.** In addition, it leads the league in average attendance at its home games (15,000).

The University of Portland's women's team won the NCAA Division I national championship in 2002 and 2005.

## SWIMMING

**Don Schollander**, who was raised in Lake Oswego, was a championship freestyle swimmer. He was a winner in two Olympics: in 1964 and 1968. He won four gold medals in 1964, and another in 1968; he also won a silver medal that year. At the 1964 Olympics, he set three world records. In 1964, he was **named as top amateur athlete in the country** by the Associated Press.

Kim Peyton, of Portland, was a member of the American team that swam in the 1976 Summer Olympics. She won a gold medal that year in a freestyle event—setting a world record. She also participated in two Pan-American games, winning a total of five gold-medals in them (in 1971 and 1975). As a youth, she set three national swimming records.

Brenda Helser, who grew up in Oregon, won a gold medal in London in the 1948 Summer Olympics; she won it in the 4x100m freestyle relay. She was a longtime member of the Multnomah Athletic Club team that between 1939 and 1948 won fifty-eight individual swimming titles at the national level; she also was on three teams that won titles. Suzanne Zimmerman was also part of that team, winning a silver medal in the 1948 Summer Olympics—for the

100-meter backstroke event. Nancy Merki was also part of that team, though she missed the 1940 Olympics (which were cancelled). As an individual, she set nineteen national records in Amateur Athletic Union (AAU) meets.

In the 1960 Summer Olympics in Rome, Carolyn Wood of Portland swam as a member of the US team, winning a gold medal in the women's 4x100m freestyle relay.

Norman Ross, of Portland, won three gold medals in freestyle events at the 1920 Summer Olympics in Antwerp. During his swimming career, Ross set thirteen world records and won eighteen American championships.

Louis Kuehn, who went to Oregon State University, also won a gold medal in the three-meter springboard diving event at the 1920 Olympics, while Thelma Payne won a bronze medal in the same event. She held the AAU title in that event for three years prior. Payne is also remembered for being the model of the diving girl in the red swimsuit that was the trademark for Jantzen swimwear.

Also winning a bronze medal at a recent Olympics was Chris Thompson, from Roseburg, who won it in the 2000 Summer Olympics in the 1500-meter freestyle. In this event and in the 1650-meter event, he set American records.

Della Sehorn set eighteen American records in breaststroke. She also was a member of the American Olympic team in the 1952 Helsinki Olympics.

### SURFING

A legendary Hawaiian surfer now lives in Bend, Oregon. George Lopez been called the "best tuberider in the world." In 1972 and 1973, he won the Pipeline Masters competition. He now manufactures surfboards and snowboards there.

### TENNIS

Turning professional in 1991, Jonathan Stark of Medford won two, top-level, singles titles and nineteen doubles titles. Among the doubles championships he won were the French Open (in 1994) and Wimbledon (in 1995). He was a member of the US Davis Cup team in 1997. While at Stanford, he was an all-American.

Emery Neale of Portland won sixteen national titles in the 1970s, including the National Senior Hard Court Singles three times. In 1969, he was ranked first nationally in the Men's 45.

As a sophomore at Stanford, Sam Lee won the 1933 NCAA Doubles Championship. In 1947 and 1948, he played in the Wimbledon doubles tournament. Phil Neer won the NCAA Men's Tennis Championship in 1921 and the doubles championship a year later. He also did this while at Stanford.

## SKIING, SNOWBOARDING, AND SLED RACING

Bill Johnson, of Brightwood, Oregon, won an Olympic gold medal in alpine skiing in the 1984 Winter Olympics at Sarajevo. In Olympic downhill events, he was the first skier from outside the Alps to win. He won three other FIS Alpine Ski World Cup downhill events that winter.

At the 1968 Winter Olympics in Norway, Kiki Cutter, from Bend, won a gold medal in the slalom. She won three other World Cup events in the slalom in 1969, and another in 1970.

In the 2002 Winter Olympics in Salt Lake City, Chris Klug, from Sisters, won a bronze medal for snowboarding in the parallel giant slalom.

**Mt. Hood's Palmer Snowfield** provides **the nation's leading place for summer skiing**, and the only one served by a lift. The area has the longest ski season in the US. It is the site of the oldest organized ski race in America, and the only summer ski race sanctioned by the US Ski Association—the Golden Rose Ski Classic (begun in 1936).

**The Mt. Bachelor Ski Resort** has been rated as **among the top five ski resorts in North America** (by *Ski Magazine*). It is on one of the few mountains on which all sides are skiable.

The terrain east of Bend is used to train huskies for sled races, like Alaska's Iditarod.

*Achievement in Sports*

### MOUNTAIN AND ROCK CLIMBING

**Mt. Hood** is **the most-climbed major mountain in the United States**, and the second-most-climbed mountain in the world (after Mt. Fuji in Japan); in an average year, 10,000 people climb it.

**Smith Rocks**, north of Bend, is **one of the best rock-climbing areas in the world**. It is the first rock climb in the US to be rated as 5.14c in difficulty (meaning it is particularly challenging).

In 1963, Willi Unsoeld, who grew up in Eugene, was a member of the first American climbing team to reach the summit of Mt. Everest. He and a partner did it from the West Ridge, in the first major traverse of a Himalayan peak. Unsoeld had often been a climbing guide on Mt. Rainier, and earlier served as a climbing guide in the Grand Tetons.

Oregon's Stacy Allison is the first American woman to reach the top of Mt. Everest (she did it in 1988).

Steven House, of La Grande, has been a professional mountaineering guide for the American Alpine Institute and Exum Mountain Guides. He has climbed in the North Cascades, the Canadian Rockies, the Alaska Range, and the Himalayas (including Nanga Parbat). He has published widely and won various climbing awards.

### WINDSURFING AND HANG GLIDING

**Hood River** is **a national mecca for windsurfing and wind-related water sports**. Specialists have said that it is "one of the greatest places for wind that there is." The largest kite school on the West Coast is also there. Floras Lake on the coast (south of Bandon) is also a popular place for windsurfing, as is the area around the mouth of the Pistol River (south of Gold Beach).

The area around Lakeview has also become a magnet for hang gliding. This activity is fostered by the region's varied topography and strong updrafts. The thermals along the 2000-foot western scarp of Abert Rim are regarded as ideal for hang gliding. Every Fourth of July, hang gliders meet there for what may be the biggest gathering of its kind in the West.

## ANGLING

The Deschutes River attracts anglers from around the world to fish for its summer run of steelhead. The North Umpqua, the McKenzie, and the Rogue are also noted for their fine fishing.

## DISTINCTIVE FISHING BOATS DEVELOPED IN OREGON:

Four types of fishing boats have been developed in Oregon, and are still only built there.

**McKenzie River dories** are now a favorite of individual rowers on the Colorado River.

They have a flat bottom; wide, flared sides; a pointed stern; and a narrow, flat bow (enough to accommodate a motor). Also they have a bottom that is arced from bow to stern (called a "continuous rocker.") They are rowed facing into rapids, with backstrokes for maneuvering to avoid obstacles.

The McKenzie dories originated in Eugene in the 1930s. They were built by Tom Kaarhus and Woody Hindman and were bought by the best guides. Martin Litton introduced them to the Colorado River.

**Rogue River longboats** also are used by commercial guides on the Colorado River.

These have a flat bottom, without a rocker shape, but an upward rake under the prow and stern. They can hold the current and have a large carrying capacity. They are not as responsive as McKenzie River dories, but are easier to row. Also they have a higher prow and a lower-profiled transom end.

The Rogue River longboat was developed by Glen Wooldridge, and refined by Bob Pritchett and Press Pyle. They are built in Grants Pass and the Gold Beach area.

*Achievement in Sports*

While dories with varied designs are now seen in Cape Kiwanda, the classic **Cape Kiwanda Beach dories** had a flat bottom, flared bow, flat stern (with fish trays), and a notched back for an outboard motor. Originally, they had double ends and a standing wheelhouse. Use of these dories here began in 1910, and later hundreds came to be launched each day. They usually seek rockfish and coho salmon.

**Astoria gill net boats** have now virtually disappeared, but they had a round bottom, a net hanging from the flared bow, and a wheelhouse in back. They were the first boats with a square stern built for Columbia River gillnetters seeking salmon in inland waters. They were fast for their time, and used from Oregon to Alaska. They were built by various Astoria boatyards.

Wooden boats such as these are celebrated each year at the McKenzie River Wooden Boat Festival, at Vida on the river.

# CONCLUSIONS

Oregon stands out in all the ways described in this book:
- because of all the things in the West that happened in Oregon first
- because of the records set here
- because of the fascinating things that have happened here
- because of its exceptional natural endowment
- because of its leadership on public policy
- because of the diversity of its specialty crops
- because of the way it has preserved and celebrated its history
- because of its prowess in sports
- because of the recognition and awards given to its music, theater, libraries, public television, festivals, flowers, gardens, food, and drink
- because of its leadership in forging a new economy

Oregon's leadership and excellence in so many different ways lift it to an even higher level in its overall distinction. A culture of striving to excel is spreading in the state. And this is particularly striking in light of the modest size of its population. It certainly stands out from the crowd.*

From the early days, Oregon has shown leadership and has often set the pace. But the state not only stands out—it is exemplary in many ways. While it is far from perfect, it is notable, and has few rivals.

Michael McCloskey | 173

## Oregon: A State That Stands Out

\* Is this idyllic state of affairs about to end? Will an overdue earthquake of stupendous size soon manifest itself? Tectonic plates offshore in the subduction zone, scientists say, may soon collide, precipitating such an earthquake.

While prudent preparations can limit the damage resulting from such an earthquake, much of the damage will be unavoidable. And other parts of the West Coast are also targeted for this "big one." Oregon is not alone in its exposure.

And other parts of the country are enduring a quickening pace of disasters that may be the result of a changing climate: unprecedented floods, waves of tornadoes, punishing hurricanes, severe droughts, and extreme forest fires. Others have to cope with these every year, rather than at 300-year intervals. And some are even suggesting that the Pacific Northwest may be the best refuge for those fleeing from all of these other troubled places.

Disasters of this type are beyond the scope of this work. They should be seen nationally in the context of climate-change policy, FEMA planning, and improved land-use planning.

True, problems of national scope continue in Oregon as in much of the country: poverty, inequality, and discrimination. But it does what it can. And the state should not be expected to solve these problems on its own.

Its thriving New Economy has developed as it has striven to meet high environmental standards. It is a fact that both now co-exist in the state. More and more of its businesses in the New Economy are pledging to adhere to various guidelines of sustainability. This suggests that the two might even have a mutually beneficial relationship.

Oregon is a place that should be celebrated. And it should continue to try to live up to the highest standards.

# SOURCES

*Cascades East Magazine. Little Known Tales from Oregon History, vol. II*. Bend: Sun Publishing, 1991.

Engeman, Richard H. *The Oregon Companion: A Historical Gazetteer of The Useful, the Curious, and the Arcane*. Portland: The Timber Press, 2009.

Frank, Gerry. *Gerry Frank's Oregon*. Salem: Gerry's Frankly Speaking, 2014.

Jarvela, Andrea. *The Oregon Almanac: Facts About Oregon*. Portland: Westwinds Press, 2000.

Loy, William G., ed. *Atlas of Oregon*. Eugene: University of Oregon Press, 2001.

Marschner, Janice. *Oregon 1859: A Snapshot in Time*. Portland: Timber Press, 2008.

McCloskey, Michael. *Conserving Oregon's Environment*. Portland: Inkwater Press, 2013.

O'Donnell, Terence. *That Balance So Rare: The Story of Oregon*. Portland: Oregon Historical Society Press, 1988.

*Oregon Blue Book: Almanac and Fact Book* (Secretary of State, 2008, Salem)

Oregon Historical Society: exhibit on WW II in Oregon (2015)

Peterson del Mar, David. *Oregon's Promise: An Interpretive History*. Corvallis: Oregon State University Press, 2003.

Pintarich, Dick, ed. *Great and Minor Moments in Oregon History*. Portland: New Oregon Publishers, 2003.

Robbins, William G. *Landscapes of Promise: The Oregon Story: 1800-1940*. Seattle: The University of Washington Press, 1997.

Warren, Stuart. *Oregon Handbook*. Chico, CA: Moon Travel Handbooks, 1998.

Winthur, Oscar Osburn. *The Great Northwest*. New York: Alfred A. Knopf, 1960.

The daily *Oregonian* and *Portland Tribune* also provided an invaluable resource for this book, as did various online sources via Google, including the *Oregon Encyclopedia* and *Offbeat Oregon*.

# INDEX

**Symbols**

41st Infantry Division 87, 89

**A**

Abernathy, Governer George 10
Abert Rim 58, 170
Adler, Leo 54
aerial tramway 47
Age of Exploration 6, 7, 8
Age of Exporation 9
Agness 31
Air Pollution Authority 67
Albany 15, 35, 94, 98, 101, 102, 118, 123, 124
American Fur Company 8
Arlene Schnitzer Concert Hall 94
Ashland 16, 34, 63, 70, 72, 94, 104, 132, 137, 139, 141, 146
Astor Column 23
Astoria 7, 8, 12, 14, 22, 23, 27, 30, 86, 88, 89, 92, 93, 94, 103, 112, 114, 139, 146, 147, 152, 172
Astoria-Megler Bridge 27
Aurora 101, 121, 141
Autzen, Thomas 113

**B**

Baker City 30, 44, 54, 93, 119, 139
Baker County 38, 106
Baker, Edward 86
Barber Block, the 96, 97
Basques 38
Beavers, the 160, 162
Beaverton 84, 117, 118, 134, 151
Bend (city) 20, 29, 36, 40, 42, 72, 73, 88, 90, 93, 94, 113, 116, 122, 137, 139, 142, 144, 146, 148, 160, 168, 169, 170, 175
Benson Bubblers 35
Benson Hotel, the 91
Benson, Simon 35, 91, 99, 105
Benton County 83, 101
bicycles 69, 137
Big Dipper (rollercoaster) 23
Bing cherry 16
Blue River 58
Boardman 89, 135, 137
Bob's Red Mill 120
Bonneville Dam 24
Borax Lake 64
bottle-deposit law 67
Brandeis, Louis 49
Broadway Bridge 46
Bryan, William Jennings 37
Burns (city) 24, 37, 138
Burnside bridge 46
Burnside (street) 31

**C**

Camp Clatsop 90
Canby 35, 77–79, 101, 103
Canemah 12
Cannon Beach 46, 63, 72, 103, 148
canoe fete, the 41
Cape Blanco 7, 27, 55, 88
Cape Falcon 7
Cape Ferrelo 7
Cape Kiwanda 59, 172
Cape Kiwanda Beach 172
Cape Lookout 7
Cape Meares 7, 61
Cape Perpetua 59
Cape Sebastian 6, 7
Cascade Forest Reserve 59

Cascade Locks 46
Cascade-Siskiyou National Monument, the 71
Cascades, the 18, 20, 57, 59, 60, 170, 175
Cathedral Park 143
Cave Junction 63
Chamberlain-Ferris Act, the 38
Chamberlain, George 34, 100
Champoeg 10
Chapman Elementary School 63
Chautauqua events 34
Chemawa Indian School, the 20
Chinese Garden
    Lan Su Chinese Garden. *See* PNW
Chinese immigration 105
Chinook 121
Christmas trees 74
Christmas Valley 60
Citizens Initiative Review 53
civic engagement 54
Civilian Conservation Corps 42
Civil War, the 32, 33, 86, 87, 102
Clackamas 27, 125, 127, 137, 152
Clackamas River 27
Clatskanie 12, 94
Cleveland, Grover 31, 41
Cloud Cap Inn 17
Collier Memorial State Park 73
Columbia College 14
Columbia Gorge 56, 71, 72, 79, 105, 121
Columbia Plateau Lava Flow 56
Columbia River 7, 8, 10, 12, 15, 20, 24, 27, 35, 56, 63, 64, 72, 86, 88, 103–105, 112, 172
Columbia River Basin 24
Columbus Day Storm 27, 99
conifers 60

Michael McCloskey | 177

Coos Bay  30, 42, 55, 66, 74, 94, 95, 113, 114, 140
Copperfield Affair  38
Coquille  20, 39, 114
Coquille River  20
Cornucopia (town)  18
Corrupt Practices Act  50
Corvallis  12, 34, 88, 90, 94, 133, 165, 166, 176
covered bridges  18
craft breweries  144
cranberries  74
Crane Union High School  23
Crater Lake  55, 57, 62, 105, 106, 148
Crescent City  12
Crooked River National Grasslands, the  59
Crosby, Bing  42
Crown Point  105
Crystal Springs Rhododendron Garden, the  64, 65
Curry County  61, 72
Cusick Mountain  61

# D

Dalles, The  12, 14, 30, 103, 119, 135, 139
Dark Horse Comics  143
Dayville  139
Debs, Eugene V.  37
Decemberists, the  143, 150, 153
Depoe Bay  64
Depression, the  25, 40, 42
Deschutes County  8
Deschutes River  36, 72, 93, 171
Diamond Crater  57
Direct Primary Law, the  49
Doerner Fir, the  61
Douglas County  61, 75
Douglas fir  8, 60, 61, 73, 113
Doyle, A.E.  35, 96, 97, 98, 116, 148
Drake Park  72
Drake Pond  42
Drake, Sir Francis  7
D River  55

Ducks, the  159

# E

Eagle Creek  18
Earp, Virgil  38
Earp, Wyatt  38
eastern Oregon  9, 12, 14, 24, 26, 30, 32, 37, 50, 57, 60, 77, 78, 86, 113, 128
Ecotrust (conservation organization)  71
Edwards, T.A.  32
electric cars  68
Elgin  28
Elk Rock Gardens of the Bishop's Close, the  65
Elkton  8, 46
Employers' Liability Act  50
Erickson's (bar)  31
Eugene  12, 13, 14, 24, 35, 37, 40, 42, 61, 69, 72, 73, 75, 84, 85, 86, 94, 98, 101, 107, 108, 116, 118, 127, 131, 132, 136, 139, 141, 142, 146, 147, 153, 158, 164, 165, 170, 171, 175
Evergreen Air Museum  44

# F

family leave laws  81
ferries  10, 35, 126
fishing  4, 27, 112, 116, 152, 171
Five-Mile Rapids site  26
flag  6, 11, 44
Floras Lake  88, 170
Florence  58
Forest Grove  15, 94, 101, 158
Forest Park  72
Forestry Building, the  22
forests  29, 32, 58, 59, 70, 76, 155
Forest Service Employees for Environmental Ethics  71
Fort Clatsop  8
Fort Dalles  13
Fort George  7
Fort Rock  26

Fort Stevens  86, 87, 88
Fort Umpqua  8
Fort Vancouver  13, 30, 66, 87
Fort Vancouver National Historic Site  13
Foster, Mary  18
Franke, Jonathan  141
Franz Family Bakery  145
Fremont Bridge  45
Frenchglen  20, 21
French Prairie  9–10, 29
Frohnmayer, Dave  53

# G

gas tax  51, 107
George Fox University  158, 162
ghost towns  18
Gilbert House Children's Museum, the  41
Gladstone  34
Gleneden Beach  148
Glenn Jackson Bridge  45
Glide  79
Gold Beach  31, 149, 170, 171
golf  116, 165–166
Goose Lake  12
Gordon, Joe  161
Grange, the  34
Grant County  58, 105
Grants Pass  21, 72, 94, 95, 121, 141, 171
Great Basin  58, 60
Great Northern Railroad  23
Green, Edith  52
Gresham  121
Grotto, the  140

# H

Hanley, Bill  37
Happy Canyon Indian Pageant, the  19
Harney County  23, 37
Harney Desert  32
Harriman Springs Lodge  36
Hart Mountain  57, 64
Hassam, Childe  32

Hawthorne Bridge  45
Haystack Rock  58, 59, 63
healthcare  81, 82
Heathman Hotel, the  91
Heceta Head  7, 21
Heceta Head Lighthouse  21
Hells Canyon  34, 55
Hermiston  77, 89
high school graduation rate  82, 83
Hill, James J.  36, 37
Hillsboro  84, 94, 122, 124, 129, 130, 133, 134, 135, 141, 151, 158, 162
H. J. Andrews Experimental Forest  59
Hollywood Theater, the  94
Honeyman State Park  43
Hood River  17, 72, 77, 104, 105, 121, 139, 148, 150, 170
Hood to Coast Relay  164
Hot Lake Hotel  57
hot springs  57
Hoyt Arboretum  60
Hudson Bay Company  8, 10, 12, 66
Hughes, Howard  44
Hvam, Hjalmar  44

## I

Imperial Ranch, the  113
Independence (town)  28
Industrial Workers of the World  38–39
initiative and referendum processes  48–49
International Rose Test Garden, the  64

## J

Jacksonville  12, 15, 16, 37, 100, 103, 139
Jantzen Beach  23
Jantzen Beach Amusement Park  23
Japanese Garden  65–66
Japanese internment  89
Jason Lee House  13
Jefferson County  62
Jefferson (proposed state)  44
John Day  24, 58, 105

John Day Dam  24
John Day Fossil Beds National Monument  58
John McLoughlin, Dr.  8, 13
Jordan Valley  37
Joseph (city)  28, 149, 150
Josephine County  61

## K

Kaiser Shipyards  113, 126
Kiger Gorge  59
Kingsmen, the  143, 152
Kinzua  18
Klamath County  36
Klamath Falls  36, 57, 64, 73, 77, 89, 94, 110
Klamath Falls Naval Air Station  89
Klamath Lake  12, 36, 56, 64
Klamath National Wildlife Refuge  17
Klootchy Creek  61
Knight, Phil  151, 164
Ku Klux Klan  39

## L

Lafayette  14, 84
La Grande  34, 94, 95, 170
Lake Oswego  15, 16, 96, 125, 163, 166, 167
Lakeview  57, 170
Lancaster, Samuel  105
Lane County  8, 13, 21, 62, 85, 87, 139
Lane, Governor Joseph  10
Lan Su Chinese Garden  66
lava flows  56–57
Lazarus, Edgar  105
Lewis and Clark
    expedition  8, 31
    Exposition  22, 23, 113
    Memorial Column  147
    Way  32
Lewis & Clark College  15, 70, 100, 157
Lincoln City  55, 94
Lincoln County  64

Linfield College  14, 158, 160, 161
Lithia Park  72
Lloyd Center, the  115
local-food movement, the  74
Lost Forest, the  60
Lost River, the  64
Lower Table Rock  58
Loyal Legion of Loggers and Lumbermen  39
Lundquist School of Business  156

## M

Madras  58, 77, 88
Malheur County  61, 62
Malheur Lake  20, 57
Malheur National Wildlife Refuge  37
manufacturing sector  109
Marion County  61
Marquam Hill  47
Martin, Charles  42
Marylhurst College  16
McCall, Tom  31, 68, 69, 72, 149
McCullough, Conde  25
McKenzie Pass  57
McKenzie River, the  171, 172
McLoughlin, Dr. John  8
McMenamin brothers  94, 119
McMinnville  44, 94, 121, 122, 124, 139, 158
McNary, Charles  42, 149
Medford  58, 74, 77, 88, 90, 94, 98, 101, 103, 116, 119, 126, 127, 128, 151, 163, 168
Meek, Joe  11
Meier and Frank  92, 95, 114
Meier, Julius  42
millraces  35
Milwaukie  12, 16, 120, 126
minimum wage  51, 53, 111
Mission State Park  61
Missoula Floods, the  56
Mitchell, John H.  46
Monmouth  28
Morse, Wayne  46

mountain men 14
Mount Angel Abbey 16, 84
Mt. Adams 72
Mt. Bachelor Ski Resort 169
Mt. Howard 27
Mt. Jefferson 72
Mt. Mazama 26, 57
Mt. Rainier 72, 170
Mt. St. Helens 26, 72
Muir, John 36
Mulkey, Philip 87
Muller v. Oregon (1908) 49
Multnomah Athletic Club 41, 167
Multnomah County 17, 61, 97, 146
Multnomah County Courthouse 97
Multnomah County Library 17, 146
Multnomah/Embassy Suites Hotel 91
Multnomah Falls 56, 148
Multnomah Hotel 36
Munson Valley 105

## N

NAACP 33
National Guard 87, 88, 89, 90
National Register 18, 20, 23, 25, 65, 91–106, 119, 147
Native Americans 9, 10
Nehalem 7
Nestucca Bay 64
Neuberger, Richard 54
Newberry Crater 57
Newport 25, 58, 75, 88, 103, 139, 140
Nez Perce 30, 32
Nike 116, 117, 164
Noble fir 60
North Bend 20, 42, 88
Northern Pacific Railroad 31
Northwest Fur Company 7
nuclear power 68, 123
Nyssa 78

## O

Oaks Park 35
Olcott, Ben 39
Old Church, the 99
Old College Hall 15, 101
Old Perpetual Geyser 57
Olmstead, John Charles 22, 102
Olmsted, John 65
Oneonta 20
Oregon and California Railroad 38
Oregon Association of Nurseries 66
Oregon Bach Festival 139
Oregon (battleship) 31
Oregon Blue Book 50, 176
Oregon Cascades, the 57
Oregon Caves National Monument 43, 57, 105, 148
Oregon Caves National Monument, the 43, 57, 105, 148
Oregon City 8, 11, 12, 13, 16, 19, 26, 36, 84, 100
Oregon Clipper. *See also* Western Shore
Oregon Coast 17, 64, 140
Oregon country, the 9–10
Oregon Department of Transportation (ODOT) 108
Oregon Electric Railway 39
Oregon Exchange Company, The 11
Oregon Fever 6
Oregon Garden, the 66
Oregon Health Plan, the 52
Oregon Health & Science University 47, 82, 128, 154, 157
Oregon Historical Society 20, 22, 29, 31, 40, 43, 74, 92, 93, 148, 175, 176
Oregonian, the 15, 117, 129, 138, 150
Oregon Indian Medicine Company, the 32
Oregon Indian Wars 30
Oregon Institute of Technology 157, 163
Oregon Institute, the 13, 157, 163
Oregon Iron and Steel Company 15
Oregon Journal, the 95

Oregon Museum of Science and Industry (OMSI) 146
Oregon Public Broadcasting (OPB) 142
Oregon Railroad Commission 50
Oregon's Coast Range 55
Oregon Shakespeare Festival 139
Oregon Spectator, the 15
Oregon Stage Lines, the 30
Oregon Statesman, the 15
Oregon State University 76, 77, 102, 124, 154, 160, 161, 162, 168, 176
Oregon Steam Navigation Company, the 20
Oregon Steamship Navigation Company 12
Oregon Symphony 94, 138, 140
Oregon System, the 48, 51, 68
Oregon Trail 6, 14
Oregon Vortex, the 43
Osborne, William Bushnell 37
Oscar Osburn Winthur 14
OSU. *See* Oregon State University
Owyhee Dam 23, 24

## P

Pacific Fur Company 7
Pacific Gas and Electric Company 68
Pacific Northwest 13, 14, 59, 115, 139, 143, 174. *See also* PNW
Pacific Railroad Survey 29
Pacific Republic of the Western States, the 10
Pacific Rivers Council 71
Pacific University 14, 15, 101, 158
Palmer Snowfield 24, 169
Parsonage 13
Parsonage, the 13
Pearson Field 43
Pelican Bay 36
Pendleton 19, 22, 88, 94, 95, 119, 121, 139, 161
Pendleton Round-Up 22
Peninsula Park 65
Pennoyer, Sylvester 31, 34, 41
People's Power League 48

Pettygrove, Francis  29
Peyton, Kim  167
Philip Foster farm  18
physician-assisted suicide  52
Pierce, Walter  39
Pinkham, Dayna  119
Pink Martini  142
Pioneer Courthouse  16, 92
Pioneer Pageant  40
Pittock Mansion  99, 100
PNW  13, 15, 16, 65, 94, 112, 148. See also Pacific Northwest
Polk County  61
Populist Party of Oregon  34
Portland  9, 12, 15, 16, 17, 18, 21, 22, 23, 29, 30, 31, 32, 33, 34, 35, 36, 37, 38, 39, 40–41, 43, 44–46, 47, 49, 52, 53, 54, 59, 60, 63, 64–66, 68, 69, 70, 72, 79, 81, 84, 88, 91–100, 101, 103, 109, 110, 113–126, 128, 132, 134, 135, 136, 137, 138, 139, 140, 141, 142, 143, 144, 145, 146, 147, 148, 152, 153, 156, 157, 158, 160, 161, 162, 163, 164, 165, 166, 167, 168, 169, 175, 176
Portland Art Museum  32, 98
Portland Art Museum, The  32, 98
Portland Baroque Orchestra  138
Portland Center Stage  139
Portland Consumers League  49
Portland Hotel, the  92, 93
Portlandia (statue)  98, 146
Portlandia (television show)  152
Portland International Airport  115
Portland Rose Festival  142
Portland Rose Society, the  64
Portland's Central School  21
Portland State University  99, 157, 160
Portland Trailblazers  163
Portland Youth Philharmonic  138
Portland Zoo  146
Port Orford  55, 61, 62, 88, 106
poverty  112, 174

Powell's Books  116
Prefontaine, Steve  150, 163
Prineville  36, 58, 135, 139
Progressive Era  48
Providence Hospital  15
"prudent man" rule, the  52
PSU. See Portland State University
public drinking fountains  35
public transportation  69
Public Utility Districts  51

## R

racism  32, 33, 34
Redband Trout Reserve, the  71
Redding  21
Redmond  37
Reed College  148, 156, 157
Reedsport  46, 139
Renninger, Louis  86
reproductive health  80
Restore Oregon  98
Rimrock Draw Rockshelter  26
Riverfront Park  72
Riverside Park  72
Riverview Cemetery  38
Rogers, Will  37
Rogue River  8, 31, 59, 61, 72, 104, 149, 152, 171
Rogue River-Siskiyou National Forest, the  59, 61
Rogue River Valley  104
Roosevelt, Franklin  42
Roosevelt, Theodore  17, 35, 37, 105, 147
Rose Bowl  159, 160
Roseburg  8, 16, 21, 73, 79, 116, 168
Rose Festival  44, 45, 65, 142
Ross Island Bridge  45
Round Barn  20
Royal Rosarians  44–45, 142
Rucker, Gabriel  145, 149

## S

Salazar, Alberto  163
Salem  9, 12, 13, 14, 15, 20, 29, 34, 35, 41, 72, 78, 79, 81, 84, 88, 94, 98, 101, 122, 127, 136, 137, 139, 141, 146, 147, 158, 175, 176
sales tax  53
SAT scores  82
Sauvie Island  8, 26, 74, 103
Scappoose  117, 122, 150
Schollander, Don  167
Sea Lion Caves  59
Seaside  32, 61, 146, 147
Second Voluntary Infantry Regiment  87
Sellwood Bridge  45
Seneca  58, 73
Shaniko  113
Sherwood  61, 127, 146
Shipbuilding  12, 33, 113, 126
Shore Acres State Park  66
Silcox Hut  24
Siletz Indian Reservation  28
Silicon Forest, the  128–132
Silver Falls State Park  43
Silverton  66, 150
Simpson, Captain Asa  20
Siskiyou Mountains  60
Skidmore Old Town Historic District  96
Skinner's Butte Park  72
Skiway Sky Bus  46
Sleater-Kinney  143, 153
Smith Rocks  170
Snake River  38
Southern Oregon University  160
Southern Pacific Railroad  39, 103
Southern Pacific System, the  16
South Waterfront  47
Spanish-American War  31, 87, 147
Spokane, Portland, and Seattle Railway  36
Spokane Portland & Seattle 700  46
Sprague, Charles  42
Springfield  76, 111
Spruce Goose, The  44

Stamp Out Hunger 85
Star of Oregon 12
Steamboat Inn 27
steamboats 12, 20, 30, 36
Steel Bridge 46
Steens Mountain 38, 58, 59, 62, 64, 71
Steens Mountain complex, the 71
Steiner, Henry 106
Stein's Pillar 58
St. Helens 26, 72, 112
St. John's 23, 45, 143
St. John's Bridge 23, 45
St. Mary's Academy 15
Sugar Pine 8
Sumpter Valley Gold Dredge 44
Sun River resort 90
sustainability 69, 113, 120, 157, 174
Swan Island 41, 78, 79, 125, 126

## T

Talbot, David 71
Talent (town) 118, 137, 166
Thorns, the 167
Thor's Well 59
Three Arch Rocks 17
Tilikum Crossing 45
Tillamook 8, 17, 21, 26, 27, 43, 61, 62, 76, 77, 88, 89, 94, 114, 121, 139
Tillamook Burns 43
Tillamook County 61, 62
Tillamook Rock Lighthouse 21
Tillamook State Forest 139
Timberline Lodge 24, 106, 148
Timbers, the 167
Toledo 39, 114
Tom McCall Waterfront Park 31, 72
Tongue Point Naval Air Station 89
Tualatin River, the 12

## U

Umatilla (city) 135
Umatilla National Forest 32, 77
Umpqua Bank 128
Umpqua River 8, 27, 36, 46, 64
Union Pacific 36, 45
Union Pacific Bridge 45
unions (labor) 34, 111, 113
Union Station 98
Union (town) 57
University of Oregon 26, 41–42, 47, 70, 81, 95, 101, 102, 113, 147, 155, 156, 159–162, 164, 165, 175
University of Portland 158, 164, 167
U of O. *See* University of Oregon
upper Klamath Basin 64
Upper Klamath Lake 12, 36
U'Ren, William S. 48
US General Land Office 11

## V

Vancouver 7, 8, 10, 13, 15, 30, 43, 66, 87, 152
Vista Ave. Viaduct 45
Voodoo Donuts 145
voting by mail 52

## W

Waldo Lake 56
Waldport 46
Walker, Jim 116
Wallowa County 8, 61
Wallowa Lake 27–28
Wallowa Lake Tramway 27
Wallowa Mountains 18, 60, 61, 63
Warm Springs 19, 32, 121
Warm Springs Reservation, the 19
Wasco County 14, 26
Washington Irving 9, 152
Washington Park 64, 147
Waterfront Blues Festival 143
Water Pageant 40, 42
Waters, Walter W. 41
West Coast waterfront strike 43
western Oregon 59

Western Shore. *See also* Oregon Clipper
Westfir 18
West Linn 26
West, Oswald 34–35, 38, 48, 51
Wheeler County 18
Whiskey Run 20
Whitman Massacre 10
Whorehouse Meadow 38
Wieden + Kennedy 116
wildlife forensics 70
Willamette Falls 12, 16, 20, 56
Willamette National Forest 58, 59, 61
Willamette River 12, 23, 35, 65, 67, 72
Willamette University 13, 14, 15, 101, 158
Willamette Valley 8, 9, 12, 29, 39, 56, 64, 77, 78, 79
Willamette Woolen Manufacturing Company 14
William Holmes House 13
Wilsonville 131, 133, 157, 165
wines 75, 144
Wolf Creek Tavern 21
Wolf Rock 58
women's suffrage 50
Wood, C.E.S. 30, 32, 35, 37, 48, 147
World War I 31, 38, 40, 87, 114, 147
World War II 24, 26, 33, 44, 46, 88, 90, 113, 114

## X

Xerces Society, the 71

## Y

Yaquina Bay Lighthouse 21
Yaquina Head 7, 21
Yoncalla 104
Young, Cal 40

## Z

Zumwalt Prairie, the 63

3/17
L

Silver Falls Library
410 S. Water St.
Silverton, OR 97381
(503) 873-5173

DISCARD

CPSIA information can be obtained
at www.ICGtesting.com
Printed in the USA
FSOW04n0313020317
31441FS